LIFE LINES

Your Final Answers to Life's Biggest Questions

ROBERT LESLIE HOLMES

Ambassador—Emerald, Intl.
Belfast, Northern Ireland • Greenville, South Carolina

Life Lines

Copyright © 2000 by Robert Leslie Holmes

Scripture references are from the *King James Version.*

Published by
Ambassador—Emerald, International
427 Wade Hampton Blvd.
Greenville, SC 29609 USA
and
Ambassador Productions
Ardenlee Street
Belfast, Northern Ireland
BT6 8QJ

www.emeraldhouse.com
www.ambassador-productions.com

To

the staff team and members of

the First Presbyterian Church of Pittsburgh family,

whose encouragement, support and love

make my ministry more effective and who

are a constant source of joy in the Lord's service.

I appreciate and love you all.

Where do I find the answers to life's biggest questions? Can I be sure they are authentic? Where do you turn when you're not sure where to turn? These *Life Lines* speak to these questions. They provide the final answers for life's biggest questions. More than that, they provide guidance for living in a time like ours. They will hold you up when you're wondering what to believe or when you reach the end of your rope. My prayer is that as you read these pages, you will find your faith strengthened and your life reinforced in good ways. If that happens, I have achieved my purpose in writing this book.

We live in an "Elijah time" and that is why this book had to be written. I call this an "Elijah time" because the glut of home-brewed systems of religious belief and new age spirituality in our generation have created an ambivalence and uncertainty not unlike that which the prophet Elijah faced on Mount Carmel. The outgrowth is that the so-called "information age" has a lot of uncertainty attached to it. The chapters in this book examine foundational life questions; they are the questions we all ask. In response, they provide solid principles, unchanging answers from the oldest faith statement known to Christians. Just as Elijah on Carmel challenged the Israelites and Baal prophets to decide what they believed and give their final answer, each chapter in this book examines the foundational integrity of the Apostles' Creed *Life Lines*. As you read these pages, you will find that the final answers to life's biggest questions are summarized in timeless principles I call *Life Lines*. They have stood the test of time. Because they are squarely based on God's word, they will continue to stand firm for as long as we live. We can count on them being trustworthy tomorrow, next year, or a hundred years from now. They provide lasting, practical solutions to our problems and our needs.

Where do I find my final answers to life's biggest questions? In time-tested, Bible-based life principles that have helped Christians survive persecution, famine, wars, calamities, sickness, brokenness, and terror of every kind, and that's what these *Life Lines* are.

Like all my other books, this one is no "Holmes alone" product. A lot of very special people deserve credit for what follows on these pages. Sometimes they receive credit in the text. Sometimes they do not. So, I mention them here. At the top of the list, as usual, is my wife and best friend, Barbara. She read every word that follows. So, when you find a typo or grammatical error blame her as much as you blame me. Blame Betty Chapman, my assistant at First Presbyterian Church of Pittsburgh, too. Betty also read all these pages long before you received them. Seriously, without these two and their constant encouragement, this book would never have made it to the printers. They each made corrections and offered suggestions that are incorporated in the text, and I owe them a debt far greater than I can repay. I am deeply indebted to Debra Meyer whose proofreading skills and encouragement once again are of special help to me. Thanks, Debra. A special word of thanks is also due to that wonderful group of people called the First Presbyterian Church of Pittsburgh. Their love and affirmation of my ministry are a constant source of blessing for me, and I am truly grateful to every one of them. Worthy of extra special honor are the members of our staff team who have encouraged and assisted me in numerous ways. I thank God for them all.

Sam Lowry and Tomm Knutson, together with all the fine folks at Ambassador-Emerald International, deserve special thanks for their patience and constant encouragement. Thank you all.

Finally, you, the reader, deserve special recognition for buying this book. Thank you. I hope its message enriches your walk with Christ and makes your life better. I send it forth with my prayer that it will be used to do just that.

The stories told throughout this text come from a variety of sources. As far as possible, I have traced down and identified the starting place of each one. If I've slipped up and repeated something you told me without proper credit, please know that the omission was not intended. If you let me know, I'll make sure you receive appropriate credit in future editions.

Soli Deo Gloria!

Robert Leslie Holmes
Pittsburgh, Pennsylvania
Easter 2000

CONTENTS

CHAPTER 1
Does It Matter What I Believe?   9

CHAPTER 2
Where Can I Find the Best Answers in the World?   17

CHAPTER 3
Is There a God?   25

CHAPTER 4
If There Is a God, What Is He Like?   33

CHAPTER 5
Where Did I Come From?   41

CHAPTER 6
Who Was The Most Amazing Person Who Ever Lived?   49

CHAPTER 7
Where Did Jesus Christ Come From?   57

CHAPTER 8
Can a Virgin Have a Baby?   65

CHAPTER 9
Who Is This Man Like Me?   75

CHAPTER 10
What Is the Greatest Love Story in History?   85

CHAPTER 11
Is There a Hell?   93

CHAPTER 12
Can We Prove Jesus Christ Rose From the Dead?   101

CHAPTER 13
Where Is Jesus Today?   109

CHAPTER 14
Will Jesus Christ Come Back to Earth?   119

CHAPTER 15
Who Is the Most Powerful Person in the World Today?   129

CHAPTER 16
What Is the One True Church?   139

CHAPTER 17
When Someone Hurts Me, What's the Best Revenge?   147

CHAPTER 18
Is There Life After Death?   157

CHAPTER ONE

Does It Matter What I Believe?

Suppose someone was to set before you a series of simple, plausible principles that would answer your biggest questions and transform your life in such a way as to help you achieve your maximum potential, jump every hurdle, and overcome every obstacle that gets in your way? What would you do with those principles?

This book sets forth a series of principles like that. These are *Life Lines*, which, if you follow them, will help you live your life on a higher plane than is otherwise possible. Read the chapters ahead and you will find answers to the questions that, sooner or later, arise in the mind of every thinking person. Knowing the correct answers to these questions will help you achieve an understanding of God that you may have only dreamed of before. Let me hasten to add that this is not because of this book's writer but because of the principles or *Life Lines* about which he writes here. Simple, succinct, easy-to-understand statements, they have been around for nearly two thousand years. They have been questioned, challenged and battered at the hands of doubters, but they have come out on top every time. They are truth; immovable reality in a complex, transient world. These are undeniable and proven life principles that will enrich life for you and enrich you for life.

We held a funeral service for Don last Saturday. As I prepared to conduct his service, I smiled about my remembrances of the first time we met. Don lived on the streets downtown and on the north side of our city. Three days before his funeral, Don somehow mixed it up with a couple of thugs who decided that Don's life was worth less than the few possessions he carried. Don was one of a number of center-city nomads who often worship with us.

Nancy Williams introduced me to Don between services on Easter Sunday morning four years ago. Nancy met Don on the street and responded to his request for help by inviting him to Easter breakfast at our church. At first, Don tried to decline Nancy's invitation. But all of us who know Nancy know that there are few things more powerful than an idea whose time has come in Nancy's mind. Don was coming to breakfast. After breakfast, he was also coming to church.

Nancy is no quitter. When she befriends a street person two things are going to happen. First, Nancy helps materially and those who ask her for assistance will receive support. Second, that person is going to be invited to worship beside Nancy and listen to the gospel of Jesus Christ, every down and outer's best friend. With her winsome ways and loving persistence, Nancy rises above every objection thrown in her pathway.

There was just one problem that Easter Sunday, according to Don. He told Nancy he felt dirty and, therefore, unworthy to enter the sanctuary. He claimed he had neither shaved nor bathed in more than a week. I suspect most of us who met him that morning would have willingly believed it was longer.

"That's not a problem for me," Nancy told him. "If it's a problem for you, we can fix it." He said it was a problem. With that, Nancy brought Don to me. "This is Don," she told me by way of introduction. "He is my guest today. I told him you would help him find a place to wash up and shave. You will, won't you?" How could I say no to Nancy?

I ushered Don to the bathroom next to my office and showed him where to find shaving cream, soap, towels, deodorant, and the other things he might need to clean up. "Be at home," I told him. Then I left.

About thirty minutes later, Don was sitting next to Nancy in the sanctuary. He was cleaned up and dressed up in a suit Nancy had requisitioned from her husband, Phil. I had returned to the bathroom to brush my teeth before the second service. I opened the bathroom closet and reached, in one swoop, for my toothbrush and toothpaste. Before I turned on the tap, a drip of cold water rolled off the bristles of my toothbrush, along the handle, and down my right thumb. Instantly I realized that Don had taken my invitation to make himself at home more literally than I intended. Yes, Don had brushed his teeth—the same ones that hadn't been brushed in at least a week—with my toothbrush!

"Faith," said J.G. Stipe, "is like a toothbrush. Everyone should have one and use it regularly, but he should never use someone else's." Don probably never heard of either J.G. Stipe or his toothbrush analogy.

This is not a book about toothbrushes but about belief so strong it can be called faith. This book speaks about the foundational Creed of Christians, the Apostles' Creed. "I believe," the Creed affirms and then it sets forth a series of tenets that millions of Christians affirm in churches around the world every Sunday. What difference does saying "I believe" on Sunday make on Monday through Saturday? This book explores the principles of the Creed and suggests practical ways to make them work every day of the week.

This is an age confused by a mixture of unbelief, uncertainty, and multi-beliefs. Our generation seems to be settling for a spiritual stew whose ingredients include belief, unbelief, and uncertainty. We are caught in a quagmire of unbelief in any god, uncertainty about whether there is a god, and belief that any old god will do. According to this mindset, what one believes about god is a matter for one to decide for oneself. If one chooses to believe, according to this train of thought, all gods are finally equal. That is why this book has to be written.

This strange concoction of atheism, agnosticism, and new-age pantheism runs loose all across the civilized world. From around the globe we are hearing that it doesn't really matter what one believes so long as we believe something. Yet, God warns, *"Woe unto them that call evil good, and good evil; that put darkness for light, and light for darkness; that put bitter for sweet, and sweet for bitter. Woe unto them that are wise in their own eyes, and prudent in their own sight!" (Isaiah 5:20,21).* For that reason, before we explore the tenets of the Apostles' Creed, we need to stop and ask some basic questions about belief.

DOES IT REALLY MATTER WHAT WE BELIEVE?

Someone said there are two ways to slip easily through life. One is to believe everything. The other is to believe nothing. Both ways save us from thinking. I believe that what we believe is very important. In fact, I believe that what we believe is of utmost importance. It is more important than who we marry. It is more important than the career we choose. It is more important than anything else we embark on in life. In fact, what we believe is a determining factor in all these things because what we believe will ultimately determine who we will become. *"For as (a man) thinketh in his heart, so is he" (Proverbs 23:7).*

When I use the word "belief," I intend it to mean what I believe the framers of the Creed accepted as its basic connotation. For them, to believe was more than to affirm something intellectually. Belief was no mere head exercise. For them, belief signified commitment. It meant being so committed to what one believes that one would risk his life for it. For the apostles and countless Christians who have followed them for about two thousand years now, believing the life principles this book explores did, in fact, cost them their lives. "The blood of the martyrs has been the seed of the church" in every generation. Living in "safe" places like America and much of Western Europe, it is easy to forget that Christians in other parts of the world suffer constantly for their beliefs.

Equally important, it is also easy in a generation like ours to miss the absolute connection between belief and behavior. Not long ago the principal occupant of the White House, having been caught up in a scandal that nearly brought down his presidency, addressed the American people with these words, "This matter is between me, the two people I love most—my wife and daughter—and our God."

"God and family!" It's a kind of necessary mantra for anyone aspiring to high elected office in the United States. Has anyone ever been elected to a national political office in America after having declared, "I don't believe in God or family?" I doubt it. The bigger question is does the person using those words really believe them? Truth is, in every instance, only God knows. The best evidence of what one really believes, according to Jesus, is how one lives one's life. *"By their fruits ye shall know them,"* he said (Matthew 7:20). So, according to Jesus, to use the words "I believe" with one's lips but deny them in one's life is not authentic Christianity. That, too, is why this book is being written.

Jesus wants us to know that true belief is the seed of action and actions are the stuff of life. Actions speak louder than professed beliefs. To really believe is to stake one's life on what is held to be true and unbreakable. It is to be willing to risk everything for life principles too valuable to be compromised. It is to step out into the unknown. As he reflected on his faith during the time soon after his wife died, C. S. Lewis said, "You never really know how much you really believe anything until its truth or falsehood becomes a matter of life and death to you. It is easy to say you believe a rope to be strong and sound as long as you are merely using it to cord a box. But suppose you had to hang by that rope over a precipice. Wouldn't you then discover how much you really trusted it?...Only a real risk tests the reality of a belief."[1]

"Abraham believed God, and it was counted unto him for righteousness" *(Abraham 4:3).* For Abraham, belief in God meant he would step away from his heritage and step into the darkness of uncharted territory. He would go where none had ever gone before. He would, in Lewis's words, take "a real risk."

BELIEVE AND ACHIEVE?

"Whatever the mind can believe, the body can achieve!" This is one of the popular phrases from the pop psychology of the self-improvement movement. Is it true? Sometimes. Sometimes, however, it is not true.

Let me give two examples. A young woman I know, Janie, is in the final stages of cancer. Her physicians have concluded that they have done everything they know to do. They have told her and her family that their treatment strategy has evolved from cure to comfort. She has not responded well to any known treatments for her disease and her condition continues to deteriorate. Therefore, they will try to assist her with pain treatments for whatever time she has remaining. She doesn't like that. She told me, "Some nights I dream that I will be healed. I even see myself at my newborn granddaughter's wedding." She added, "I look healthy!" She says she believes God can make her well again and I believe she believes that. I believe it, too. I have no choice. In the course of my ministry I have encountered a number of people who are walking evidence of the fact that it is never wise to give up. However, both Janie and I also know that reality calls for a two-track strategy at this point. If she lives, praise the Lord! If she dies, she is prepared. So, believing she can be healed, Janie has placed herself in the hands of Jesus. For her, "Whatever the mind can believe, the body can achieve" is just a chorus. It is not necessarily reality.

On the other hand, consider Dr. Ben Carson, one of the foremost pediatric surgeons in the world today. This son of black-ghetto poverty has risen to the top of his profession in the elite world of pediatric neurosurgery. His reputation for successfully separating Siamese twins is known around the world. Children from across the globe are brought to him for treatment. In his early schooling, Ben Carson was no shining star. He grew up in poverty and looked as though he were headed for a life far from the elite halls of medicine. But something happened. What was it? Ben Carson would tell you that the grace of God intervened in his life, and he began to believe he could be more than it looked like he would be. He applied himself to his studies, went through medical school and post-graduate training that prepared him for a career on the front tip of the cutting edge of pediatric surgery. It would never have happened had he not first believed. If you want evidence that "whatever the mind can believe, the body can achieve," you likely would not find a better example than Dr. Ben Carson. Before we can achieve any great thing, we have to believe it is possible.

BELIEVE AND BE AND LIVE

Have you ever played with anagrams? An anagram is a word or series of words formed by reordering the letters of another word. One anagram of the word believe contains two words: "be" and "live."

Those two words are, in fact, the foundation of what I believe the framers of the Creed believed when they gave us these life principles. To "believe" is to "be" and to "live" what we profess to believe. Faith helps us to *be* a Christian. Only Jesus Christ in the Holy Spirit's power can make us *live* like one. Abraham had to live out what he believed.

THE BIG G AND THE LITTLE G

It was politically prudent for the President to affirm his belief in God. To profess belief in God is probably still a necessary prerequisite for a long-term successful career in just about every area of public life. The fact remains that a married man who participates in a sexual relationship with a woman about the age of his daughter and vehemently denies that relationship when challenged is not living out belief in the God of the Bible. In this case believe and "be live" are at odds. Life and lip do not match. His plight is not at all uncommon in America and around the world.

Two deities are vying for the soul of our nation and our world. These two seem also to be in contest for our individual souls. One is the big G, God. This is the God of the Bible who is known, as he wants to be known, only through his Son, Jesus Christ. The other is the small g, god of our own imaginations. This is a toy deity who can be played with at whim and put away when he becomes a bother, and who turns a blind eye to our misdeeds and wipes our sin-slate clean at our convenience.

Not long ago I was invited to offer an opening prayer at a major civic function in downtown Pittsburgh. As I see it, such an invitation always provides an opportunity to speak a word for Christ. Therefore, I accepted the invitation with some degree of enthusiasm. At the appointed hour, I was on the dais all prepared to make a brief prayer. A printed program listed me as a participant right next to the word "Invocation." It seemed like an easy assignment, but I was in for a jolt.

Imagine my surprise a few days later when a rather sternly worded admonition came from an officer of the inviting organization. He informed me that I had violated a bylaw of the organization by mentioning the name of Jesus in my prayer. I was shocked and taken aback not only by what he wrote but also by the tone in which he wrote it. My choice of words obviously had angered him. In no uncertain terms, his letter indicated that I should have known better. It implied that I intentionally violated a principle. That was not true. "It is not that we do not believe in God," the writer noted, "but that we don't believe it is right for someone to stand up in one of our meetings and make reference to his or her idea of God because we do not want to offend people of other faith groups."

I got the message. It was political correctness taken to its final extreme. I was supposed to park my personal belief in God revealing Himself in his Son, Jesus, outside the door and make a to-whom-it-may-concern statement that would fail to offend a plethora of unspecified deities—sort of just speak into the air and hope that no one's god would be offended, and that the right god would pick up my innocuous prayer and act favorably upon it. In short, I must set my big G God on the shelf or leave him at my office, and pray to all the small g gods whose devotees might chance to hear.

As I reflected on that experience, my mind was drawn back to the encounter between Elijah, the prophet, and the devotees of the Baals on Mount Carmel when the once-great nation called Israel found itself divided both politically and spiritually. *"How long halt ye between two opinions?"* Elijah challenged them. *"If the LORD be God, follow him: but if Baal, then follow him." (see 1 Kings 18:21).* It was a call for them to make up their minds about life's biggest question, about whether they would follow the big G God or a host of little g gods.

COSMO VERSUS CHRIST

Here is another example: In the turbulent sixties, Helen Gurley Brown, then editor of *Cosmopolitan* magazine, raised a voice for loose morality with her book *Sex and the Single Girl.* Not long ago a senior writer for a leading Christian periodical wrote, and a "religious" Internet site published, an article called *Sex and the Single Evangelical.* In the article the young woman openly acknowledges her own sleep-around habits. She chides her friend who challenges her to consider the Bible's strong prohibition against such a lifestyle, responding that the evangelical church is in denial about its sexually active single adults. It is her way of saying, "Everybody's doing it." In other words, personal experience and peer pressure should be allowed to trump Scripture and 2000 years of Christian teaching. She even goes so far as to claim for herself a higher moral ground because she is open and honest about her lifestyle, and presumably she believes her friend is not.

The question she is facing in her own way is the same one we all are faced with nationally and personally. It is not whether we have a small g, god or gods, but whether the God who created us and redeemed us in the sacrifice of his Son, Jesus, has us.

"With the heart man believeth unto righteousness; and with the mouth confession is made unto salvation. For the scripture saith, Whosoever believeth on him shall not be ashamed" (Romans 10:10,11). Are you investing your life in places where the large G, God of the Bible, is not welcome? To believe as the human authors of this Creed intended us to believe is not

only to make a confession of the lips but also to back up our confession with our lives.

AMERICA'S ELIJAH GENERATION

What happened at that meeting between Elijah and the Israelites is similar to where we are, and where we seem to be headed, spiritually in America. Elijah challenged the Israelites to see that in their quest to satisfy a plethora of false and phony deities they were, in fact, offending the only true God, the One who created the universe, delivered them from bondage in a strange land, and guided them home. America is in a time like that now.

A late afternoon tornado forced two amateur explorers traveling through a dense forest to find shelter in a cave. After the tornado had howled past them they emerged to a terrifying sight. Huge trees that not long before had provided them with markers now lay uprooted and broken like rough kindling. Familiar landmarks that they planned to rely on to find their way home again were obliterated. Every mark they had made to help them retrace their steps was erased and lost among the rubble. They were filled with such a sense of lostness that one of the men sat down on a log and wept. "We are lost," he cried. "We are not lost," his friend responded. "Soon darkness will come and we can find our way by the stars. The stars are not lost. Therefore, neither are we." He was right. Long before the compass was invented, ancient mariners found their way across the oceans and around the world by the stars. The stars never move. They can be relied upon to show us the way in the darkness.

What we need in our Elijah generation are some firm answers, life principles that will not be moved or changed, that will stand the test of time, and deliver us home safely. Those life principles are found in the oldest Christian Creed known. Even though it may not be the direct work of the apostles, it is called the Apostles' Creed. Since the second half of the second century A.D., this Creed's principles have proved that time cannot erode them. What is more, they are the basis of all the other creeds in Christian history. Together these principles form the backdrop for what is written in the pages that follow. So, come with me and discover principles that will enrich your life in ways you perhaps have never imagined as we follow these *Life Lines,* your final answers for life's biggest questions. Read on and come alive!

CHAPTER TWO

Where Can I Find the Best Answers in the World?

If someone presented you with a fountain of truth that had survived well over a millennium of challenges and came through intact, would you believe it?

CHECKING OUR SOURCE

"Always double-check your source!" A newspaper editor made that statement often to his cub reporters each year. Hard experience had taught the editor that, given enough time, an unreliable source will almost always be undermined and, if the newspaper prints information from such a source, the newspaper's credibility will suffer. "Always double-check your source," he said.

It was good advice. It is always wise to consider our sources and especially to know whether a source is reliable. That is never more important than when we are determining which principles will guide our lives. Therefore, the purpose of this chapter is to determine whether the *Life Lines* that are presented in the chapters that follow will hold. In the words of an old hymn, "Will your anchor hold in the storms of life?" That is a question well worth asking before life's storm clouds appear, which inevitably they always will.

The U.S. Postal Service released a stamp promoting the Grand Canyon as part of a new millennium collection. On the first printing, every single stamp noted that the Grand Canyon is in Colorado rather than Arizona. When someone brought this to the attention of the stamp's printers, they responded by saying they would do a reprint. In the second printing, the picture of the Canyon was printed in reverse. The west side of the Canyon appears to be the eastern side and the eastern side is pictured as though it is the west side. After the second error was pointed out to the Postal Service, a decision was made to let it stand because few people would notice the difference.

Errors like that manage to get into print on a daily basis. Check any major newspaper. Often there is a regular "Corrections" column. The sole purpose of the corrections column is to rectify errors printed in previous editions. Sometimes errors are not spotted for a long time. Sometimes no one "notices the difference." When that happens, misinformation is often perpetuated as reliable truth. A popular middle school history book said that Napoleon Bonaparte became Emperor of France in 1769, which was actually the year of Napoleon's birth. Hundreds of history teachers relayed 1769 as the year of his ascendancy to their students, some of whom perhaps perpetuated this misinformation to subsequent generations.

In chapter one, I said that the Apostles' Creed is the oldest creed of the Christian faith and the foundation for all other Christian creeds. All of this is impressive. Yet, none of it by itself should be sufficient for us to blindly accept the Creed at face value. Therefore, before we explore the Creed's *Life Lines*, it is important to understand where they are rooted.

THE SWAMPY GROUND OF UNCERTAINTY

Albert Schweitzer is reputed to have said that it is impossible to build a city of truth on the swampy ground of uncertainty. By the same token, a life should not be built on what we cannot be sure will stand the test of time. Schweitzer was not the first person to advise us of this truth. Jesus was, when he cautioned us against building our house on sand (see Matthew 7:26). Before we can truly mean it when we say "I believe," we need to be certain that what we believe will not sink beneath us when the life storms come our way. Why did the Creed authors choose their particular *Life Lines* as foundations for successful living? Why only these and not others? What was the bedrock of their profession? Where was their anchor grounded? The answer to each of these questions: the Bible. Every line in the Creed communicates a solid Bible principle.

This recognition begs the epistemological question: "Is the Bible reliable?" It is obvious that if the Bible is not trustworthy, if it is a "swampy ground of uncertainty"—to borrow Dr. Schweitzer's words—then what is built upon will also be suspect.

TRUTH TRIED – A PERSONAL TESTIMONY

It seems appropriate at this point to come clean. There was a time in my early ministry when serious doubts about the Bible's credibility almost directed me to pursue a career in law or psychology instead of attending seminary. As an undergraduate student, I came under the influence of certain theologically liberal teachers.

Personal experience at that time indicated that these teachers were not evil people. They were, I now believe, merely misguided. As a result, they were also misguiding: "The blind leading the blind." Therein lay the real danger. Having said that, it is important to say that the love and caring they demonstrated toward me greatly impressed me. When I speak of them now I do not do so with any malice. My heart's desire is for them to find the peace in Christ I have found. That peace is only found where there is certainty about all God's promises. Because of their loving spirits, it would have been easy to accept what they said at face value. They called into question many passages of the Bible including the Genesis creation record, the virgin birth of Jesus, his atoning work on Calvary's cross, his bodily resurrection, and the Second Coming. You can see right away that each of these is a foundational tenet of the Apostles' Creed. My teachers' doubts about the validity of these basic Bible teachings caused me to question whether I could preach anything from the Bible with life and death conviction. I realized that I was not a good enough actor to deliver an untrustworthy message with conviction. I was a very idealistic young man and there was nothing I wanted less than to be a hypocrite who preached one message and believed another.

Months of personal Bible study and research, heart searching, and seeking the counsel of trusted friends brought me to the conclusion that the Bible not only is believable but that of all the books I had ever read, the Bible is in a class by itself in terms of credibility. I determined it would be the bedrock upon which my life would be founded.

No one was more helpful in directing me to this conclusion than my uncle, Sam Heslip, under whose guidance I had received Christ and sensed my initial call to enter the gospel ministry. His words echo once more in my mind as I write them here for you. "The Bible," he said firmly, "is not a book to argue about, but to live by." He recalled how the Bible has always had its critics but that no one had ever discredited even a single passage of it. He concluded by challenging me to take the Bible and its message at face value until someone proved unequivocally that something about it was not credible. "Don't be afraid," he said, "to put the Bible through a credibility test. You will find it still stands when all its critics have passed away."

Accepting the premise of my Uncle Sam's challenge became one of my life's watershed moments. Something within me told me that I was on the right track. I believe it was the inward whisper of the Holy Spirit. I was, in the apostle Paul's words, *"strengthened with might by his Spirit in the inner man" (Ephesians 3:16).* As my Uncle Sam's challenge began to take root inside me, I sensed that the battle for truth that had raged in my mind for months had been won and that the victory was God's. I relate this experience now only to acknowledge that I did not always subscribe wholeheartedly to the view of Scripture I espouse today.

THE BIBLE'S BEST FRIEND

"The word of the LORD is right; and all his works are done in truth" *(Psalm 33:4).* The Bible is reliable because God's word is never untrue. God never forgets. He does not miscommunicate. He never twists his words nor leaves promises unkept. This is all part of his unchangeable nature. Everything he does is trustworthy for all time.

"Time may be a great healer," Lucille Harper said, "but it's a terrible beautician." She realized that time does things to people that not everyone likes. With time's passing, skin loses its firmness and teeth need to be replaced or repaired. Hair is lost with time, as is the nimble nature of youthfulness. Time plays havoc with our health, our strength, and our looks. Time is indeed "a terrible beautician." Yet, time is also the Bible's best friend. With time's passing, the Bible looks better and better. Part of the proof that the Bible is reliable is that time always works on its side and allows its truth to be confirmed with new discoveries in archeology. If the Bible were not true, we would expect that at some point modern archeological findings would contradict its message. Yet, the opposite has happened. Many of archeology's recent findings have served only to further enhance the Bible's credibility.

When others question parts of the Bible, we do not need to defend its message before them. "The Bible is not a book to argue about, but to live by." Simply bid them to wait a while. In time all their questions will be answered and the Bible's authenticity will stand.

Of the thousands of books published each year throughout the English-speaking world, less than one percent survive for seven years. The Bible, however, not only has kept people's interest for centuries, it is the number-one seller each year in bookstores. Hardly anyone would consider re-reading a classic ten times, yet many people read the Bible through every year for decades and testify that each year they find fresh and precious truths that serve to make their lives richer. How can this be? It can only be because the Bible is alive with the Spirit of God.

GOD'S BREATH

"All scripture is given by inspiration of God, and is profitable for doctrine, for reproof, for correction, for instruction in righteousness: That the

man of God may be perfect, thoroughly furnished unto all good works" (2 Timothy 3:16,17). In my book *The Breath of Abundant Life,*[2] I make note that only three times does the Bible mention God breathing. This is one of them. Speaking of God's inspiration of the Bible, the apostle Paul combines the strength of two Greek words to make *theopneustos. Theos* means God. *Pneustos,* from the same Greek root as our English word pneumatic, means air and implies air under pressure, such as in a pneumatic tire or in breathing. For Paul there could be no doubt. God exerted his breath over each human author of the Bible. Using the unique personality and writing style of each writer, God gave the world a book that would never be equaled as long as the universe stands. It is wholly reliable because God's breath is upon it.

THE LAMPLIGHT

Robert Louis Stevenson was a sickly child. He spent much of his childhood in bed because of lung trouble. Even though he died when he was only forty-four, his stories, poems, and essays have been an inspiration to millions of readers. One story about him echoes from his Edinburgh childhood. It reports the night his father entered Robert's bedroom and found the young boy staring out the window. "What are you watching?" Robert's father asked. "I'm watching the lamplighter punching holes in the darkness," Robert replied.

"Thy word is a lamp unto my feet, and a light unto my path" (Psalm 119:105). God's word punches holes in the darkness, too. Wherever it has traveled around the world, its light has pierced the darkness. Theodore Roosevelt said, "Every thinking man, when he thinks, realizes that the teachings of the Bible are so interwoven with our whole civic and social life that it would be literally impossible for us to figure what life would be if those teachings were removed. We would lose almost all the standards by which we now judge both public and private morals; all the standards towards which we, with more or less resolution, strive to raise ourselves."

That is, no doubt, why the framers of the Apostles' Creed stayed with the Bible when they committed their beliefs to writing. They knew that a creed founded on any other source would not withstand the onslaught of the years. On a trip down a coal mine in Beckley, West Virginia, our guide demonstrated how, before the days of modern mining machines, each man harvested his daily sixteen-ton ration. "His biggest fear was that his lamp might go out and he would be left in total darkness," our host said. His words reminded me that Europe fell into the historic Dark Ages largely because the lamp of Christ was allowed to go out. By God's grace, however, the spark for new light was already laid in the Irish monasteries. From there, the Irish missionaries set out to re-evangelize Europe, making preparation for the Middle Ages and the Renaissance that turned the direction of a continent around.

On a personal level, millions would testify to the Bible's unique ability to provide direction when life is perplexing and the way ahead looks dark or cloudy. When we lived along the Gulf Coast, a group of men took a small boat to one of the islands several miles offshore. They were having so much fun that no one noticed the dense and unexpected fog that was falling over the water. By the time they realized what was happening and gathered their belongings to head back to the mainland, they found themselves engulfed in a pea-soup fog. Seeing even a few yards ahead was next to impossible. Fortunately, one of them carried a small compass that was part of his Swiss army knife. He took it from his pocket and with a tiny light was able to discern the direction of its needle. What he saw defied his sense of direction. In spite of that, he and his companions agreed they would follow what the compass told them. From time to time one of them would shout out above the noise of the boat motor, "I think we're headed in the wrong direction." Each time, out came the compass and the light. Finally they caught sight of the lights of their hometown harbor. With unbelievable precision, they were back exactly where they had started their journey. The Bible is like that, too. There are times when the way seems unclear. At times like that, God's light still shines. You can trust it.

God's light will never go out for us when we trust him. *"Unto the upright there ariseth light in the darkness" (Psalm 112:4).* Jesus promised, *"Till heaven and earth pass, one jot or one tittle shall in no wise pass from the law, till all be fulfilled" (Matthew 5:18).* It may seem as though the fog will swallow us. But with the truth of God's everlasting light guiding us, we will always find our way home. Sometimes the journey will be made one step at a time. That step is the step the Bible calls the step of faith, or belief.

THE TRUTH ABOUT THE TRUTH

In one of the most nerve-racking encounters in human history, God's only begotten Son stood nose to nose with Pontius Pilate, the chief representative of Rome in Jerusalem. As Jesus and Pilate faced each other, the truth question met a foundational challenge. Jesus affirmed, *"To this end was I born, and for this cause came I into the world, that I should bear witness unto the truth. Every one that is of the truth heareth my voice." Pilate saith unto him, "What is truth?" (John 18:37,38).* Pilate asked Christ what we regard as an uncomplicated question but Jesus did not answer. It was not because he did not have the answer. Instead, the Son of God knew that if Pilate had any real concern for truth he would see it plainly in the circumstances that brought about their meeting. Pilate already had demonstrated that pursuit of truth was not a priority on his agenda. The high ethical and eternally consequential sense in which Jesus presented the truth was far above the horizons of Pilate's low ethical and moral standards. Pontius Pilate was a politician of the worst kind. For him, truth was a relative thing determined by popular opinion. It was in keeping with his operation to set truth aside temporarily when a situation seemed to warrant it. For him, truth was subjected to the political impulses of the moment, even if it meant a good man would die for things he had not done. For Pilate and the people he represented in Jerusalem, truth was a mere toy to be bandied about in word games and semantic gymnastics. Pilate's world measured truth by majority opinions and statements skillfully crafted to advance the cause of the moment. Relative truth like theirs cannot deal head on with a concept of "truth, the whole truth, and nothing but the truth, so help me God."

It should trouble us all that the world we live in often treats truth like that. In our courtrooms and political capitals, people make careers out of writing double-talk sentences designed to sound as though they mean one thing but which can be twisted to mean something altogether different when it seems expedient. One such encounter was demonstrated in a widely broadcast response to a simple question during an under-oath deposition. "It all depends on what your definition of is, is," the respondent said.

THE REAL REALITY

Bible truth is not at all like Pilate's truth. *"Sanctify them through thy truth: thy word is truth" (John 17:17)*. This was Christ's final great affirmation of God's word, prayed in the Garden of Gethsemane moments before Pilate's cohorts captured him. When the Scripture writers speak of truth and when Jesus speaks of truth, they mean that truth is a very final thing. It is the ultimate reality, the final standard of one's being. Its synonyms are words that leave no wiggle room. Integrity! Authenticity! Guarantee of constancy! The unchanging basis for security for all eternity! The real reality that never goes away! *"The grass withereth, the flower fadeth: but the word of our God shall stand for ever" (Isaiah 40:8)*. God, says Isaiah, has created something that will stand as a monument to everlasting truth. We call it the Bible.

Jesus was not the only one who believed the Bible to be uniquely and finally true like that. More than two thousand times the Old Testament writers affirm their certainty that the Bible is inimitably God's own word. They confirm this belief in phrases such as, *"This is what the*

Lord said," "The word of the Lord came to..." or "God said." When they say these things, they not only affirm their own belief about the Bible, they also put the authenticity of the Scriptures on the line. All it would take to undermine the whole book would be one person to prove beyond a reasonable doubt that the Bible is not believable.

The prophets, likewise, give us proof that the Bible is totally believable. Writing, often several hundred years in advance of things actually occurring, they are able to foretell with uncanny accuracy certain major events and happenings.

It is no wonder that the framers of the Apostles' Creed believed the Bible to be true. They found within it both guidance and a Guide. And they found it needs no "Corrections" column in later editions. Instead, they discovered here the prescription that remedies sin through the death of Jesus on the cross. Here they found their comfort for trial and distress. Here they met inspiration to conquer every handicap and overcome every obstacle they faced in life. Here they uncovered their map to God's presence in heaven. Here they met their Savior and their only hope of eternal life. That is why they made the Bible the source book for these life principles they passed along to us.

The Bible-based *Life Lines* that the creators of the Creed found trustworthy are still good. You will find that they are good for you.

Augustine of Hippo testified that when he searched for truth on which to build his life a voice called him to take up the Bible and read it. He obeyed that voice and his life was transformed in wonderful ways. Yours will be, too, when you follow his example. Take up the Bible and make it your life's companion. Learn its words and practice its principles. "Be" it and "live" it, then you, too, can say with integrity, *"I believe..."*

"Always double-check your source," the editor told his cub reporters. He was right. "It is impossible to build a city of truth on the swampy ground of uncertainty." Come with me now and explore the secure foundational *Life Lines* for victorious living in confusing times. In the pages ahead, you will rediscover the principles on which you can build a solid life.

CHAPTER THREE

Is There a God?

Did you ever yearn to know someone who will bring you that sense of personal security, confidence, and inner peace that comes from being certain that no matter what you have done you are loved and accepted? I believe that every human being ever born has an insatiable desire to know someone like that. How do turtles get on top of fence posts? Read on and you will find the one who puts them there.

FROM WAIKIKI TO CALVARY

Francis was our tour bus operator when Barbara and I first met him on the island of Oahu in Hawaii. His father, a Japanese Buddhist, and his mother, a Californian Roman Catholic, gave him a name that hinted at this mixed heritage. Francis Nakasone enlisted in the United States Army during World War II. Uncle Sam's Army sent Francis to Camp Shelby near Hattiesburg, Mississippi, for initial training. His eyes were intense as he admitted, "I was scared like never before because I knew I might be posted to the European front and never see my parents again."

One day, the clear blue Mississippi sky captured Francis' imagination. "It reminded me of my beautiful Oahu and how I love it," he said. "Instantly, I knew that someone very big and wonderful made these things. I looked up from an open-air shower stall and shouted towards the sky, 'Whoever you are that made my beautiful island, please keep my Mom and my Dad safe until I see them again.'"

Francis smiled. "Do you think I'm silly? Many times I have wondered if anyone really heard me." He paused and smiled again. "Reverend, what do you think?" I assured Francis that he was heard and that someone did create the Oahu sunset and the wide Mississippi sky. Francis beamed with joy. "I knew it," he exclaimed. I told him that there is something even more amazing than Oahu's sunset. It is that we can live in a personal relationship with the One who made the beach and made us. In his heart, Francis traveled from Waikiki Beach to Calvary's cross where that Someone Francis suspected was there for so many years demonstrated a love that would protect Francis throughout eternity. That day, on Waikiki's shores, Francis invited God's Son, Jesus Christ, to be Lord of his life.

LIFE'S FINAL QUESTION

How do you know that you exist? How can you prove that you are real? These questions sound silly, don't they? You know you are real because you are!

Here is another question. It is the great searching question of the ages: Is there a God? Or, is there not a God? It has long been a source of amazement to me that the Bible never attempts to prove God's existence. It simply assumes he is. *"In the beginning God,"* it says and goes on to record what God did without trying to prove his reality. Why? I suspect it is because God is so real no thinking person could ever question his existence. In a sense, we know he exists in the same way that we know we exist. Our whole tenor of life and thought is affected by our perception of God and who he is.

I TROUBLE

Who is the Supreme Being in our lives? Is it us? Are we, each of us, the utmost one? A look at the shelves in the self-help section of any bookstore would lead us to believe that. These book titles seem to indicate that there is among us a strong desire to be king of a world of one. That is not new. Since Adam and Eve, the god of self has always been one of this world's idols. A healthy self-image is a good thing. There is no honor for God in putting ourselves down. Ethel Waters said, "God don't make no junk." She's right! You are not junk. None of us, however, can afford to miss the vital difference between a sense of our God-given worth and an ego inflated by pride.

"How art thou fallen from heaven, O Lucifer, son of the morning! For
thou hast said in thine heart,
'I will ascend into heaven,
I will exalt my throne above the stars of God:
I will sit also upon the mount of the congregation, in the sides of
the north:
I will ascend above the heights of the clouds;
I will be like the most High' " (Isaiah 14:12-14).

Self-worship made a devil out of an angel. Whether Isaiah's words apply to Satan or Sennacherib (and Bible scholars have differing opinions), the fact is they betray a certain character flaw against which we must all discipline ourselves. Five times in these verses the first personal pronoun "I" leads off self-promoting ambition.

A television news documentary told about a North Carolina hog farmer whose animal waste ran unchecked into a nearby stream. Questioned about this practice, he said, "I'm smart enough not to live downstream from it." That, too, demonstrates "I" trouble. It is another way of saying "Me first."

One of the marks of this postmodern era is that it judges the value of life by personal feelings and emotions. It is the religion of "me-ism." We see the evidence of it everywhere from rap music and modern art to the new age religions. Its focus is what it does for me.

It is ultimately no different from the challenge Elijah addressed on Mount Carmel. The Baal prophets Elijah opposed built their followings by appealing to this base self-centeredness in human nature. Their problem, and ours, is that feelings are often fickle and our sense of what it takes to satisfy us constantly changes. Isaiah demonstrated that no matter how frantic feelings are, they cannot produce fire when you need it.

For the same reasons, postmodernism falls short because its only reality is a constantly moving target. The truth is that the ultimate reality exists outside us until we invite him in.

A sidewalk florist was having a terrible business day. No one was buying his flowers and he wondered if he would sell any flowers that day. Suddenly a brilliant marketing strategy came to him. He printed a sign that said, "Wearing a rose will make you look important all day today!" Immediately sales picked up. People bought roses for their lapels because people love to believe other people think they are important.

In the church, too, a theology of "me-ism" often displaces theism. A poll of congregations searching for a pastor and pastors searching for a different congregation revealed that for many congregations the primary goal was finding someone to "serve us," "build us up," "preach us good sermons," and "visit us." "Us-ism" is, of course, only a plural form of me-ism. On the other hand, the seeking pastors' chief ends included finding congregations to assist their professional advancement and position them for a "bigger call." Each of these mindsets betrays its own unique form of "I trouble." It reveals a tendency to pursue the small g god of self rather than the big G God of the Bible.

SOMEONE SUPERNATURAL

Ask yourself, who is the most important being in my life? Is it you? Or, the One who made you? If it is the latter, is he an object to be feared or revered? When you think of your most important being, are you filled with alarm, or guilt, or an overwhelming sense of being loved?

ALMIGHTY ANONYMOUS

Francis Nakasone's story took my mind back to a time in the history of Greece when a plague rampaged ancient Athens. It claimed thousands of lives. In an attempt to satisfy angry deities, whom they were certain were causing this scourge, the Athenians erected an altar to every known god in the Graeco-Roman world. The plague did not stop. Finally, in desperation, one more altar was erected. On it, these words were inscribed in large letters, *"TO THE UNKNOWN GOD" (Acts 17:23).* Somehow, soon after that, the epidemic waned. As a result, people began to pray to this new anonymous deity.

On his second missionary journey, Paul stood on Mars Hill and, noting this inscription, seized the moment to bring his listeners face to face with this God who made them and with his desire to be known and worshipped. *Whom, therefore, ye ignorantly worship, him I declare unto you" (Acts 17:23).*

LIFE LINES

The first *Life Line* passed down to us in the Creed is that God is knowable. *"I believe in God."* Let me tell you why you must believe in him, too.

THE GOD WHO IS

Everything about this universe we live in is finally a giant index finger pointing toward God: *"The heavens declare the glory of God; and the firmament showeth his handiwork" (Psalm 19:1).*

For Francis Nakasone the wide blue Mississippi sky and the Hawaiian sunset were compelling evidence that God exists. They declared to his heart that there is a Source of life and splendor. Just as Robinson Crusoe saw a footprint in the sand and knew at once that he was not the only occupant on his island, so by the same logic God has left his footprints all across the heavens and the earth.

The design, complexity, and consistency of the world force us to conclude that there is a God and that he can be known. The entire universe testifies to the existence and glory of an all-powerful Creator.

In a lead article entitled *Science Finds God, Newsweek* magazine reported a recent trend in science: Increasing numbers of scientists from diverse fields are seeing God's footprints on their discoveries. Personal testimonies from a number of leading scientists say, "I believe in God."

Dr. Charles Townes received the 1964 Nobel prize in physics for discovering the laser. He testifies that recent cosmological discoveries reveal "a universe that fits religious views" and that "somehow intelligence must have been involved in the laws of the universe."[3]

The founder and first director of the Goddard Space Center, Robert Jastrow, writes, "For the past three hundred years scientists have been scaling a mountain of ignorance, and as they pull themselves over the final rock, they are greeted by a band of theologians who have been sitting there for centuries."[4]

CHANGED LIVES

It is not only science that testifies to God's existence. A woman contacted her classmates in preparation for a twenty-fifth high school reunion. Several classmates had been out of touch with each other for a quarter-century. "I can hardly wait to see you again," she told one in a long-distance telephone call. "Oh," he replied, "you won't recognize me. In school I was straight As. Now I'm all Bs: bifocals, bridgework, baldness, bunions, and bulges!" She laughed. Another classmate wrote, "I'm looking forward to showing everyone how much I've changed. Everybody knew I was the class tramp. I had no moral standards and I graduated pregnant with a baby whose father I could not identify for sure. I left town ashamed, but now it's time to come home and show everyone what God has done in my life."

God's ability to transform human hearts through his Son is a second reason to believe in him. *"The heart is deceitful above all things, and desperately wicked: who can know it?"* Jeremiah wept *(Jeremiah 17:9)*. Who can change a rotten heart? Only God can: *"A new heart also will I give you, and a new spirit will I put within you: and I will take away the stony heart out of your flesh, and I will give you an heart of flesh" (Ezekiel 36:26)*.

Some years ago Charles Bradlaugh, an avowed atheist, challenged H.P. Hughes, the leader of a London rescue mission, to a public debate on whether God exists. Hughes knew Bradlaugh to be a skilled orator and debater. Hughes took the invitation on one condition: "I will accept if I can bring with me one hundred men and women whose lives have been changed for the good by God and you will bring one hundred people who can tell how they are helped by their lack of belief in God." At the appointed time, H.P. Hughes waited at the planned venue. One hundred men and women waited with him. They included former thieves, drunks, and street fighters. Bradlaugh was a no-show. The meeting scheduled to be a debate about whether God exists became a worship and praise celebration as one after another of the men and women gathered spoke about the change God had made in their lives.

George Wallace knew about that change. First elected Alabama's governor in 1962, he led his state with an iron hand and words that stirred up fear and hatred. When federal troops attempted to integrate Alabama's public schools, Wallace stubbornly declared, "Segregation now! Segregation always! Segregation forever!" His pugnacious face became a symbol for racial hatred and intolerance across America. His real problem, however, was not his face. It was his heart. In the late 1970s, God gave George Wallace a new heart through an encounter with Jesus Christ. Almost immediately, George Wallace invited leaders from Alabama's black community to a meeting. He told them what God had done in his heart and asked for their forgiveness. He lived out the rest of his life working for racial reconciliation. Under his leadership, Alabama became a model of what God can do through one changed heart.

In every neighborhood, including yours, there are men and women who will testify to the transforming power that believing in God brought about in their lives. You will meet them in the churches.

Charles Colson, a tough-guy Marine veteran and cutthroat lawyer, proudly wore the title "Nixon's hatchet man." He boasted, "I'd walk over my grandmother for the President." After he was convicted for his part in crimes that almost toppled the United States government, he had an encounter with God through his Son, Jesus Christ. It transformed Charles Colson's whole philosophy of life. Today his ministry has touched thousands of prisoners and their families.

GOD'S SURPRISES!

As a pastor in a church, I often see the difference God can make in lives that once were headed in the wrong direction. Through the years I have heard about marriages saved, love rekindled, tempers cooled, alcoholics and drug addicts delivered, and people healed of diseases for which medicine knows no cure. People sit in the pews of our churches on any given Sunday who should be dead. They are, each of them, proof God is alive and working in the world today!

A neurological surgeon told me, "In my work, I often see God's surprises." He recounted a number of cases where patients of his defied the known rules of medicine against all odds.

The world is full of God's surprises. Many of them are people who defied the odds and rose over circumstances that almost certainly aimed at a different outcome. Perhaps you are one of them. When I was nine years old, a rare form of facial paralysis hindered my speaking ability so much that schoolmates made fun of how I spoke. Words I had been able to say easily were suddenly beyond the range of my speaking ability. A medical specialist told my parents that I would most likely always have a speech impediment. His words echo in the ears of my heart often when I represent Christ in some part of the world neither that doctor nor I ever expected me to see. By God's grace, I, too, am one of God's surprises.

THE TURTLE ON THE FENCE POST

Bob Lamont, one of my predecessors at First Presbyterian Church of Pittsburgh, once told me, "If you ever see a turtle on top of a five-foot fence post, you know that he did not get there by himself. Someone must have put him there." I identify with that because, although Bob was not speaking about me at the time, I am like that turtle! The fact that God called me to be a messenger boy for his Son is another surprise. I can think of no one less likely, nor less worthy, to represent Christ than me. Yet, I know that God has placed his hand on my life and I can no more stay silent about his grace through Christ than the sea could keep from being salty.

I am not alone. There are millions of Christians with similar stories about God's amazing power. Perhaps you are one of them. If so, do not stay silent. Tell your story at every opportunity to everyone who will listen. Which brings me to another reason we should believe in God.

THE PROOF OF YOU

"In him we live, and move, and have our being; as certain also of your own poets have said, 'For we are also his offspring'" (Acts 17:28). How can I know God exists? While I am not God, and never can be God, I am living proof that God exists. So, too, are you. You are alive, are you not? How did you get to be alive? If, in response to that question, you were to begin to describe for me how procreation occurs out of a sexual relationship inside or outside marriage, I would be forced to stop you because your answer would be, at best, shortsighted. I would ask you to explain for me how two chemical elements can come together in that relationship and take on life. To believe that can happen without God's divine intervention is surely the height of absurdity. Recent findings in the field of DNA scream out at every person ever born that God is alive and it is not reasonable to not believe in him.

Similarly, if you were to recount for me in terms of an evolutionary process that began as a single-celled amoeba and gradually evolved into humanity, I would say that believing in God should be no problem for you inasmuch as it takes more faith to believe in neo-Darwinism than it does to believe in God. Certainly the evidence for God far surpasses the evidence of evolution in every way. Moreover, you still would not have answered the question of how life began. To believe in life without belief in God is absurd at best. *"In him was life; and the life was the light of men" (John 1:4).*

THE ONLY WAY TO KNOW GOD

"God, who at sundry times and in divers manners spake in time past unto the fathers by the prophets. Hath in these last days spoken unto us by his Son...the brightness of his glory, and the express image of his person" (Hebrews 1:1-3).

Once in all human history, God came to Earth in a unique way. This tiny planet of ours was exposed to the unquenchable light, power, majesty, holiness, and grandeur of God in his Son, Jesus Christ. In Christ, God took on flesh and blood like ours and was personal, real, touchable, and undeniably believable. The wonder of life is that in our time God can still be known and believed through Jesus. That was Paul's message for the Athenians. It was also God's message that day on Waikiki for Francis Nakasone. Today it is God's message for you if you have never believed him.

"Ye shall seek me, and find me, when ye shall search for me with all your heart" (Jeremiah 29:13). The God we believe in, as Christians, is accessible to ordinary people like you and me through Jesus. We shall see this truth more clearly in the chapters ahead.

To believe in God is simply to take him at his word; that is, to trust the promises he makes in his word and to act upon them as though they were true, even when we doubt them. This is believing as the framers of the Apostles' Creed meant us to experience it. It involves both the mind and the heart. It is both to "be" and to "live" the reality of God so that we may know firsthand a level of security, confidence, peace, and love that is found nowhere else in the universe.

In the next chapter, we will discover even more of the wonder and majesty of this God who is alive and intimately interested in each of us. Read on.

CHAPTER FOUR

If There Is a God, What Is He Like?

What difference does it make which god I believe in? Aren't we all going the same way in the end? What kind of god do we believe in? Is our deity subject to the popular opinion polls or our personal momentary passions? Is God interested in me? Read on and find out.

As long as we live, we will address no more important question than what we believe about God; that is, what kind of God we believe in. When Elijah challenged the people of Israel to come to Mount Carmel with their Baal prophets, it was not because that generation of Israelites was godless. Nor, was it that they did not believe in Elijah's God. It was that they were confused about what they really believed. They had a lot of answers but they had no final answer, no fixed star by which to guide their lives and control their actions.

SPIRITUAL COCKTAILS

The Israelites Elijah addressed were spiritual people. They had many gods (small g). Their most popular gods were called Baals. The word Baal is Canaanite in origin. It signifies, "lord," "master," or "owner." The appeal of the Baals was alluring because they allowed for diversity among their followers. The Baals took on many forms, which usually were dictated by local customs or the momentary passions of the flesh and lustful imagination of the individual person. The most prevalent symbol of the Baals was a raging bull, representing strength and sexual prowess.[5] Other images among the Baals focused on amassing power, money, popularity, and prestige.

In addition to this assortment of Canaanite gods, Asherah, the Assyrian fertility goddess, also had a large following among the Israelites, especially among the women.

Ahab, the wicked king, encouraged this religious diversity among the people. In this diversity of deities Ahab found his strength. It was a philosophy of "live and let live" taken to its extremes. So long as Ahab, the king, removed all restraints from the people, he held power through a coalition of the followers of this strange assortment of deities. The prophets of Jehovah, on the other hand, spoke out against this ancient new ageism. They knew that monotheism, the worship of one God, was what set Israel apart from all the other nations. They also knew that so long as Israel followed only the true God, they would be protected and blessed by his sovereign hand. Ahab did not oppose Jehovah; he held to a philosophy that said Jehovah was one among many gods. In time, the people formulated their own gods by blending whatever elements of the Baals, Asherah, and Jehovah they found to their own liking. Elijah, recognizing that the God of Israel demands absolute allegiance and refuses to be an also-ran among other gods, issued his challenge for the prophets of Baal and Asherah to gather on Mount Carmel. There they would decide no less a question than whom they should worship and serve. It was a day for final declarations.

It is not hard to see the parallels between Elijah's Israel and the western world in our generation. A British radio talk show host invited his listeners to create their personal religions. One caller said, "It is impossible for me to understand how any thinking person can devote his or her life to a single religion and expect to find the answer to all their prayers from one source. I do not doubt that Jesus Christ was the Son of God, but I believe that God also has many other sons and daughters. I like to create a sort of spiritual buffet of my own so that I can take whatever bits and pieces from the various religions, and some I've created myself, to suit my needs."

Such a philosophy of religion sounds very warm and alluring. Just imagine, it promises, you can make your own god! You can choose the ingredients that suit your personal fancy and sense of need. You can mix a kind of weird spiritual cocktail with only the ingredients you want. That mindset does not, at least on the surface, call us to rail against the God of the Bible or his Son, Jesus. Yet, at this very point lies its greatest danger. There are many voices calling for our spiritual allegiance today, and the cleverest among them are wily enough to know that successfully building a following is easier if they find ways to accommodate whatever sense of God we may already have. This is why I call these "Elijah times."

GOD'S IMMUTABILITY

One of my favorite authors, Chuck Swindoll, gives us an example of this mentality in a critical real-life moment. He writes about a flight on a New York-bound airliner in 1968: "It was a routine flight, and normally a boring affair. Descending to the destination, however, the pilot realized the landing gear refused to engage. He worked the controls back and forth, trying again and again to make the gear lock down into place. No success. He then asked the control tower for instructions as he circled the landing field. Responding to the crisis, airport personnel sprayed the runway with foam as fire trucks and other emergency vehicles moved into position. Disaster was only minutes away.

"The passengers, meanwhile, were told of each maneuver in that calm, cheery voice pilots manage to use at times like this. Flight attendants glided about the cabin with an air of cool reserve. Passengers were told to place their heads between their knees and grab their ankles just before impact. It was one of those I-can't- believe-this-is-happening-to-me experiences. There were tears, no doubt, and a few screams of despair. The landing was now seconds away.

"Suddenly the pilot announced over the intercom: 'We are beginning our final descent. At this moment in accordance with International Aviation Codes established at Geneva, it is my obligation to inform you that if you believe in God, you should commence prayer.'

"I'm happy to report that the belly landing occurred without a hitch. No one was injured and, aside from some rather extensive damage to the plane, the airline hardly remembered the incident. In fact, a relative of one of the passengers called the airline the very next day and asked about the prayer rule the pilot had quoted. No one volunteered any information on the subject. Back to that cool reserve, it was simply, 'No comment.'

"Amazing. The only thing that brought out into the open a deep-down 'secret rule' was crisis. Pushed to the brink, back to the wall, right down to the wire, all escape routes closed...only then does our society crack open a hint of recognition that God just might be there and—'if you believe...you should commence prayer.'" [6]

WHEN THE ICE GETS HOT...

We were invited out a few years ago for dinner with a group of people, including a professed agnostic whose family background was Jewish. We had not met him before that evening. At the restaurant, he ordered oysters on the half-shell. The oysters were delivered on a bed of dry ice. Being from another country, he had seen neither oysters nor dry ice before. After sampling an oyster, the agnostic picked up a piece of dry ice with his bare fingers to inspect it. As soon as he did, it burned him. "Oh, good Lord, save us," he exclaimed. Another member of our company who knew the fellow's professed agnosticism smiled, "There's nothing like hot ice to shake the unbelief out of folks who believe like you, is there?" It was a humorous incident that revealed a profound truth. In some ways, that experience was not dissimilar, although on a smaller scale, to what happened on that airplane.

We can try to rationalize God out of our schools, out of our public forums, out of our textbooks, and out of our national life, but we cannot rationalize him out of our crisis. Most of all, we will never rationalize him out of our death. That is something that many devotees of the choose-your-own-god club seem not to think about. In a nutshell, they fail to reckon with God's God-ness. If God is God and there is nobody like him, we do well to realize that he will have no part of being one among many choices.

It was in such an environment that Elijah called for the people to make up their minds as to whether they would follow Jehovah or a small g god. He wanted them to recognize that the God who is there and who can do anything has plans and standards that do not change at whim and will not be compromised to accommodate the latest finding of public opinion research. It was an all or nothing situation. Elijah was calling them to realize that when we cast our lot with Jehovah we gain everything, but if we don't we lose it all.

GOD'S FATHERHOOD

For the framers of the Apostles' Creed, he is "God, the Father Almighty." Any father worthy of the title will not attempt to demonstrate his love for his children through spineless permissiveness. God's expectation of us is unwavering, obedient allegiance. *"For this is the love of God, that we keep his commandments: and his commandments are not grievous" (1 John 5:3).* God, our Father, sets safe limits on us. We, who are fathers and mothers, should do no less for our own children. To allow children to run unrestrained is to sin against them and God by becoming co-dependents to their latest yearnings. It is to put them in the driver's seat of their lives before they have reached the necessary age and level of maturity to assume that responsibility. *"What son is he whom the father chasteneth not?" (Hebrews 12:7).*

Judy, a young woman at a church where I was speaking on the West Coast, told me that she could not appreciate God's fatherhood because she had an unsatisfactory relationship with her earthly father. She went on to tell me that her dad died and "left us with nothing" when she was in grade school. She had bought into the modern pop-psychology assertion that says that a poor regard for one's earthly father always results in a negative understanding of God. In response, I expressed sorrow for her sad loss and tried to show her that her statement does not stand up under close examination because it allows secular thought, and not Scripture, to set the agenda in our relationship with God. Such an approach minimizes God by bringing him down to a human level. I told her about my mother's family, whose dad died suddenly when they were small. The oldest child was fourteen years old and the youngest was but twenty months. There were six children in that family, each of whom demonstrated a healthy relationship with God and each of them, in his or her own way, bore a witness that impacted my life and drew me closer to Christ.

Both the Old Testament and the New Testament provide us with a picture of God's fatherhood. Human fathers fail miserably. I'm a father and I know that first hand. There is a Father who is love personified. He is perfect in all his ways. He is "God, the Father Almighty." In Hosea 11, God is pictured as a father who never fails his children, providing for and protecting them even when they fail to follow him, and disciplining them out of love. The picture of a father that Jesus gives us in the parable about the prodigal son is one of a father who waits longingly when his child abandons him. Saint Paul gives us a word picture of a father who adopts sinners and treats them exactly like his only true son (see Romans 8:14-17). John writes that God as our Father is not just the model of ideal fatherhood but of our own loving behavior (see 1 John 5:1-3). God is not just like a father; he is a Father, the Father Almighty. Where earthly fathers fail or are sometimes taken from us, he is always with us.

THE FATHER'S PROTECTING EYE

After the blizzard of 1993, I heard about a young boy from our neighborhood who wanted to attend his friend's birthday party when the storm was at its worst. The heavy snow and driving winds made streets almost impassable. The boy's dad at first urged him not to go to the party. In response to his son's pleas, the dad finally relented. "You may go," he said, "but please be careful." The young man wrapped his gift then wrapped himself against the elements. He lunged into the driveway and trudged along the street. A journey that usually took only a few minutes took almost a half-hour that day. Finally, he reached his friend's home and rang the doorbell. His friend opened the door and, after the two boys greeted each other, asked, "Who is that behind you?" For the first time, the young boy who had plodded through the snowstorm looked around and saw his dad retreating back through the snow. That dad had followed his lad's every step to be sure he arrived safely. He watched him all the way.

God does that, too. *"The eyes of the LORD run to and fro throughout the whole earth, to show himself strong in the behalf of them whose heart is perfect toward him" (2 Chronicles 16:9).*

THE FATHER'S UNWAVERING LOVE

A seriously ill Christian in our congregation spoke with me about her experience of doubts and fears as her health declined. "As my illness progresses," she confessed, "I find it harder and harder to have faith. Now, I'm afraid that perhaps God has stopped loving me because I don't always love him."

"When I visit my granddaughters, Hannah and Cameron," I told her, "I always go with great expectations that they will welcome me warmly and they almost always do. However, once in a while, something else is on their minds. At times like that, we joke about Barney or whoever has their attention being more important than Papa. Do I love them less because they are distracted from me for the moment?" I paused. She smiled and said, "No, I'm sure you don't." "Exactly!" I said. "My love for them is not measured by their expression of love for me, even when I'm second to Barney." In the same way, God loves us not because we have loved him first but because he is our loving Father. His love never wavers.

THE FATHER'S READY ACCESS

Coming out of President Abraham Lincoln's life is a story demonstrating how available God is to his children. An elderly American waited outside the White House hoping to speak to the President about a special need in his son's life. His eyes filled with tears as he thought of his son's predicament. He asked the White House guards if he might speak with the President, but they replied that the President was not available to everyone who came to speak with him. Presently, a young boy came along and, noticing the man, asked why he was there. The old man told that lad his story. "I know the President would help my son," he said. "He has a son of his own. He understands the love of a father." The young boy smiled and said, "I'll take you to see President Lincoln." "You?" the old man said in unbelief. "Yes, Sir," he replied. "You see, President Lincoln is my father. I can talk to him any time I want and he likes to meet my friends. When I tell him you're my friend, he'll help you." Sure enough, the old man saw the President and received the help his son needed.

As believers, we too have access to the Father. He is always available to us because we are his Son's friends. He, too, always has compassion on us when we bring our needs to him. *"As a father pitieth his children, so the LORD pitieth them that fear him" (Psalm 103:13).* In each of these ways, through his protecting eye, his unwavering love, and his ready access, God demonstrates his interest in us.

GOD'S BIGNESS

We often hear that the President of the United States is the most powerful man in the world. Therefore, we are not surprised that President Lincoln was able to help that man's son. God is more powerful than even the President of the United States, however, for even Presidents have limitations to their power. God's power is limitless. He is "the Father Almighty." That is, he is the Father without limits.

That was something Israel's Baal followers failed to grasp. They attempted to blend a strange spiritual cocktail of Jehovah and their false gods. In our desire for political correctness, we often do that, too.

Dietrich Bonhoeffer became a World War II Christian martyr because he understood God's bigness. When other church leaders of his generation turned a blind eye to Nazi terrorism, Bonhoeffer refused to go along. Instead, he raised his voice against Hitler's forces. As a result, he was put to death in a prison camp only a few days before the war ended. In a letter smuggled out of the prison, Dietrich Bonhoeffer wrote, "Only those who obey truly believe and those who believe truly obey."[7] He knew that a big God, like the God of the Bible, would not want his disciples to make peace with evil leaders, whether in government or church, because he expects and deserves absolute obedience. Moreover, Bonhoeffer feared, *"not them which kill the body, but are not able to kill the soul" (Matthew 10:28).* He believed that Almighty God would still reign on the throne of the universe long after the Third Reich had passed into oblivion.

CHEERING FOR BOTH SIDES

Elijah had a similar conviction. That is why he boldly challenged the followers of the false gods on Mount Carmel: *"How long halt ye between two opinions? If the LORD be God, follow him: but if Baal, then follow him" (1 Kings 18:21).* Elijah called the Israelites to "be" and to "live" as Jehovah's followers instead of practicing the "both/and" form of religion of their own imaginations.

A fan of the Pittsburgh Pirates, our hometown baseball team, told me about a fellow who sat near him at Three Rivers Stadium when the Pirates were playing against the Atlanta Braves. No matter which team made a hit or a home run, the fellow cheered. Finally, an inquisitive fan asked him why he rooted for both teams. He replied, "Well, I don't get to see live professional baseball very often. I root for both teams so that no matter who wins I can tell my friends that the team I cheered for won."

PREFERENCES VERSUS CONVICTIONS

Sound silly? It's not any sillier than when people who call themselves Christians around believers act like pagans around unbelievers. Their behaviors betray the fact that they are practicing preferences over convictions. There is a distinct difference between the two. A preference is a belief held temporarily until certain circumstances cause someone to change it.

A conviction, on the other hand, is a belief that will not be changed. It is a God-given firmness of position that pays no heed to the voices of popular opinion polls.

Audrey, a youth leader in her church, said she believed God was calling her to become a missionary in a developing culture. After her friends spoke of the strange foods and customs in that part of the world, Audrey began to waver. Later her family dissuaded her from leaving home with the promise of a new car. She demonstrated preference but not conviction.

Dan said God was calling him into the ministry. When he heard it would take him seven years to complete the educational requirements for ordination, he mumbled something about that being too long and changed his mind. He had a persuasion but not a conviction.

Dietrich Bonhoeffer's peers ignored Nazi brutality because their beliefs were persuasions but not convictions. They were negotiable depending on the changing winds of outside circumstances. Bonhoeffer's beliefs were convictions. They were not up for grabs even if it meant he must give his life for them.

The kind of belief the framers of the Apostles' Creed call us to is conviction. We hold fast to these life truths no matter what happens. We are convinced beyond a shadow of a doubt that God is not just a Father but he is "the Father Almighty." The final proof that we believe in him as Father Almighty comes when, like Dietrich Bonhoeffer and the first disciples of Jesus, each of whom died for their faith, we yield our will to him no matter what it may cost us.

In the next chapter, we will see this Father not only as our unfailing Father but as the Creator of the universe. Read on and know him better. Who knows, you may even change your mind about how you think about the whole world.

CHAPTER FIVE

Where Did I Come From?

Would you change the way you think about yourself if you knew that your life bears God's fingerprints? Would knowing that make a difference in how you live and how you relate to other people? Would it change the lives of our children? Read on and find out...

NOT ONE OF US!

Three monkeys sat in a coconut tree,
Discussing things as they're said to be.
Said one to the others, "Now listen, you two,
There's a certain rumor that can't be true:
That man descended out of our noble race.
The very idea is a disgrace!

No monkey ever deserted his wife,
Or starved her babies and ruined her life.
And you've never known another monk
To leave her babies with others to bunk!
Or to pass them on from one to another
'Til they scarcely know who is their mother.

And another thing you'll never see,
Is a monk build a fence 'round a coconut tree,
And let the coconuts go to waste,
Forbidding all other monks to taste.
Why, if I'd put a fence around a coconut tree,
Starvation would force you to steal from me!

Here's another thing a monk won't do,
Go out all night and get in a stew,
Or use a gun, or club or knife
To take some other monkey's life.

Yes, man has descended—the ornery cuss—
But, brother, he didn't descend from us!

—Unknown

HOW DID IT HAPPEN?

No subject in our time influences our perception of the world and of human relationships more than the issue addressed by that Creed line declaring God as the "Maker of heaven and earth." It hangs as a backdrop to almost every major concern in American education. Did God make the world and its people? Or, did it all happen by chance?

It is not stretching the truth to say that two competing religions are in a wrestling match for the soul of every child in America. The one that wins the soul of each child will determine to a large degree how that youngster views almost all of life including him or her self, other people, and the universe as a whole.

When we experience and ponder the world we live in, thinking people sooner or later arrive at the question of how it all came to be. It is this most basic question about life in our universe that gives birth to the two competing religions. The first religion is biblical Christianity, which is the sum and substance of the Apostles' Creed and its *Life Lines* that give birth to this book. The second is neo-Darwinism, the philosophy of the evolutionary principles that are assumed as fact in much of public America. These evolutionary principles were first widely published in Charles Darwin's book *The Origin of the Species.* The essence of Darwin's thesis about evolution has been modified only slightly with the passing of time, hence the name neo-Darwinism.

The first religion is founded upon *"The faith which was once delivered unto the saints" (Jude 3).* The second is founded upon a notion that has taken on the credibility of established fact with many people. It has become a vehicle for *"turning the grace of our God into lasciviousness, and denying the only Lord God, and our Lord Jesus Christ" (Jude 4).*

Among scientists who believe in evolution there is some serious debate and deep division. Principal among these are the evolutionists who subscribe to microevolution, that is, the idea that genetic changes occur within species. Biblical creationists have no particular argument with the microevolutionists, because nothing in the Bible contradicts this

42

position. Moreover, we can see the evidence of it even in our own families. Children tend to have the general appearance of either one parent or the other, or a combination of both. These are genetic realities. There are also some environmental ones. For example, studies show that children born in America of parents who emigrated from Western Europe tend to be taller than their parents or their European cousins. This is most likely the result of the American diet and other factors related to the American lifestyle.

On the other side of the evolutionary argument are the adherents of macroevolution, or the notion that species evolve into new species. Some macroevolutionists believe that these changes are spontaneous and sudden. Others believe that they come gradually over long periods of time. Why would there be this disagreement even among those who believe in macroevolution? The answer is in part because neither side can prove its case through the use of credible evidence.

Consider the other alternative again. The framers of the Apostles' Creed profess belief in God as "Maker of heaven and earth." Why should we accept what they wrote almost 2,000 years ago and reject the idea of evolution as taught by proponents of neo-Darwinism?

SCIENTIFICALLY BANKRUPT

First, we see evidence in favor of a God-created universe by the fact that evolution is scientifically bankrupt in its foundational principles. Suppose I began the Preface to this book by writing "This book will call you to build your life on a belief system that is unproven and that cannot be proved." Would you invest your hard-earned money in a book like that? Or, suppose your pastor began each sermon by declaring "Today I want you to give your life to a notion that is not proved and is not provable." Would you give your life to that idea? Would you even return to church the next week? Probably not!

That, however, is the foundation that proponents of evolution want to press upon children in America's public schools. When they do, they seem to lose sight of the fact that there is far more evidence to contradict their ideas than there is to support them. Even foundational principles of science contradict the notion of evolution.

Think of some examples. The first principle of thermodynamics says that in any closed system energy is neither created nor destroyed. That is, everything that ever was still exists in some form. For example, you fill your car's gas tank with gasoline. The gauge on the dashboard reads "F," for full. You drive for a while. Now the needle on the gauge drops near "E," for empty. The tank that once was full now has lots of room for more fuel. Where did the fuel go? The answer is, of course, that what you pumped into your tank earlier as liquid now exists as unseen gaseous fumes in the atmosphere. Neo-Darwinism, on the other hand, says that some things still happen out of nothing.

The second principle of thermodynamics declares that physical things that are left untouched tend toward disintegration. I like to visit the ruins of the ancient buildings that dot the Irish landscape. What once stood as someone's pride and joy, now lies as a collection of rubble and ruins. Those ruins demonstrate the second principle of thermodynamics. Left untended, they fell apart. However, according to evolutionary thinking, if you leave things alone they will improve.

Here is a prime example of how the principles of neo-Darwinism say life came to be: A slimy single-celled creature left the water and became a crawler. Later it emerged through a series of changes that simply happened. At one point it became a flying creature like a bird. At another time, it was a walking creature like a fox. By chance, it later developed the ability to walk on two feet like a monkey. Later that much-evolved once-single-celled slimy creature accidentally developed an opposable thumb like a person.

It does not make good scientific sense to believe in evolution because it is scientifically bankrupt.

LOGICALLY BANKRUPT

Now, a diehard evolutionist might cry "time out" at this point! He or she would point out that, in fact, there are examples of lower systems developing into higher systems. The best example of this is a seed, which, given enough time and the right circumstances, will become a fruit-bearing plant. That is correct. We all know plants grow from seeds. However, growth and evolution are not synonyms. What is more, left alone in the right environment, seeds always develop into plants like the ones from which they came in the first place. Apple seeds do not produce tomatoes or oranges. Dandelion seeds produce dandelions not rosebushes.

The same principle is true in the animal world. When male mice create seeds, or sperm, and they connect up with eggs, or ovum, from female mice, more mice are born. They will not become cats or rabbits or fish. All of nature and the latest findings in the world of DNA demonstrate that like produces like. The truth is that the notion of evolution is not only poor science, but it is poor logic.

THEOLOGICALLY BANKRUPT

Evolution is not just scientifically and logically bankrupt, it is also theologically bankrupt. It has no room for the big G God of the Bible. Instead, it worships a small g god of its own imagination called "chance."

Evolution and the biblical creation are incompatible and mutually exclusive teachings that ultimately force us to choose one or the other. Whereas the Bible says, *"Thou art worthy, O Lord, to receive glory and honour and power: for thou hast created all things, and for thy pleasure they are and were created" (Revelation 4:11),* evolution says, "Everything that exists was created by chance."

PSYCHOLOGICALLY BANKRUPT

Does evolution as it is taught in America's public schools have an impact on how we feel about ourselves? Does it influence the way our children think about themselves? Does it make any difference whether we teach them the evolutionary ideas of how they came to be or the biblical creation ones? Actually, it makes all the difference possible to a child's sense of self-esteem whether the child believes himself or herself to be a roll-of-the-dice by-product of some very ancient slime followed by a string of animals or to be created in the image of God for a positive relationship with him through His Son, Jesus.

Solomon writes, *"Train up a child in the way he should go: and when he is old, he will not depart from it" (Revelation 22:6).* Let's paraphrase that verse positively and negatively to illustrate the difference teaching evolution and creation each make to a child's sense of self-worth: *"Train up a child to believe he is the latest link in an animal chain, and when he is old he will act like an animal."* That is what evolution does. Imagine the impact of that on the behavior of schoolchildren, and you soon begin to understand why students can carry out the Columbine massacre and other similar horrors.

Now, apply the same verse to relationships and let's see the difference it makes in how we think about other people. *"Train up a child to believe his peers are animals, too, and he will relate to them as animals relate to each other."* Does that sound far-fetched? During the impeachment hearings that stemmed from President Clinton's sexual improprieties, a television psychologist, offered the notion that since we are really animals and since in the animal kingdom males often dominate females, the President's sexual indiscretions were not especially abnormal. In other words, if the animals do not control their behaviors in relationships neither should we. The speaker seemed unable to see that taking this logic to its natural conclusions means we can also justify violence, promiscuity, and drug use in our families and schools. Evolution is not just bad psychology it is terrible psychology! No wonder the monkeys in the opening poem said:

Yes, man has descended—the ornery cuss—
But, brother, he didn't descend from us!

Now, positively paraphrase Solomon's words about raising children: *"Train up a child to believe he is the prize of all creation and that child will strive to be and do the best he is capable of being and doing."*

When we train up our children to believe that they and their peers are created in God's image, we should expect that they would treat others with respect, dignity, and a sense of holiness. A child who is taught that both he and his peers are created to be stewards of life on Earth will demonstrate reciprocal grace and service.

Creation is good psychology for precisely the same reasons that evolution is bad psychology. When we understand that all of life is God's and that he has made a gift of it to us to use for as long as we live on earth, all life becomes important and worth saving. [8]

This is why we need to affirm boldly that we "believe in God the Father Almighty, Maker of heaven and earth." Three times in the first chapter of Genesis we read about what God created:

"In the beginning God created the heaven and the earth" (Genesis 1:1).

"God created great whales, and every living creature that moveth, which the waters brought forth abundantly, after their kind, and every winged fowl after his kind: and God saw that it was good" (Genesis 1:21).

"God created man in his own image, in the image of God created he him; male and female created he them" (Genesis 1:27).

Creation in Genesis chapters 1 and 2 is very well ordered. When it is broken down day by day we realize it makes sense. For example, before God made the animals and created the first man, he created the land and vegetation as a means of sustaining and supporting them. Before he made the land and vegetation, he first made light that would be necessary for repeated chlorophyll formation and reproduction. There was nothing random about it. Moreover, in addition to showing us that the world is built according to a plan, it also tells us some things about this God the Father Almighty we believe in. First, it says that our Father is creative. Second, it says he is in control of everything in His world. Third, it tells us that everything has its purpose. Fourth, it tells us that he values us highly.

The common Hebrew verb in these three verses from Genesis 1 is *bara,* which means to create directly. That is to say, when God created *"the heaven and the earth"* plus *"every living creature that moveth"* and *"man in his own image,"* he did so directly. His fingerprints are on each part of what he made. Creation is good science, good logic, good theology, and good psychology for precisely the same reasons that evolution is bankrupt in these areas. Because an orderly God made all things in an orderly way, there is good reason to honor everything about his creation. Moreover, Genesis teaches us that after he created each thing God assessed it and called it "good." He saw its value. After God made man, he called his creation *"very good" (Genesis 1:31)* because now his plan for the world was complete. God was pleased with what he made. If you have ever had the satisfaction of making something or assembling a jigsaw puzzle, you can identify with that. At about the same time, God demonstrated his over-riding purpose in making human beings. It was that we should *"be fruitful, and multiply, and replenish the earth, and subdue it: and have dominion over the fish of the sea, and over the fowl of the air, and over every living thing that moveth upon the earth. And God said, 'Behold, I have given you every herb bearing seed, which is upon the face of all the earth, and every tree, in the which is the fruit of a tree yielding seed; to you it shall be for meat'" (Genesis 1:28,29).* ***In other words, God gave us dominion over the rest of creation. We are, in effect, God's managers, the vice presidents of God's world.

Will believing this make a difference in how we view the world? Of course it will. The marvels of creation will fill our hearts with wonder and gratitude for the Creator and all he has done. Everything from sunrise to sunset will become more meaningful and joyful for us. The moon and stars will seem to shine more brightly than before. Equally important, we will assume responsibility for our environment and we will spend our lives in praise of the One who caused it all to be.

This is how Scripture views our world.

This God, the "Maker of heaven and earth," has placed us in his ordered world as vice regents, or overseers. Through Christ, he says to you and me, *"Occupy till I come" (Luke 19:13).* If we adopted this life-view, we would not only have a higher regard for our contemporaries and ourselves, we would stop throwing trash along our highways and polluting our oceans. The trees and plants, the stars and the moon would take on a new meaning, for we know God made them and charged us with taking care of them until he comes again in his Son, Jesus. We would become keepers of God's earth and teach our children the importance of appreciating this world with which God so graciously gifted us.

THE WONDER OF THE PEANUT

George Washington Carver understood the world like this. He liked to tell his story about asking God to help him understand all there is to know about the universe. Dr. Carver said, "The Lord replied, 'George, the universe is too big for you to understand. Suppose you let me take care of the universe and you find something more your size to understand.'" Humbled by that idea, George Washington Carver said he replied, "Lord, right now I feel about the size of a peanut." He said the Lord responded, "Now, George, that's a lot closer to your size than the whole world. You go to work on the peanut and I'll show you some things." As a result of that life philosophy, Dr. George Washington Carver discovered more than three hundred useful products that can be made from one tiny particle of God's creation. What a mighty Father! What a wonderful world!

CREATION: OUR BEST HOPE

"Thou shalt love the Lord thy God with all thy heart, and with all thy soul, and with all thy strength, and with all thy mind; and thy neighbour as thyself" (Luke 10:27). The truth, according to God's word, is that God made you and God made me. Moreover, he declared his good intentions for each of our lives. We discover the highest purposes for which we are made and the fullness of life for all people only as we yield our selves completely to him.

This is the final eternal difference we discover when we realize we are not the latest link in a happenstance chain of events but the best design the Architect of all creation ever dreamed of. We came from God and unto him one day each of us shall return and give an account of what we have done with these lives he has entrusted to our care.

Neither evolutionist nor creationist can prove how the world began for none of us saw it happen and none of us is capable of repeating the great experiment that brought it all about. There is one thing, however, that we can prove. It is that Jesus died to pay the penalty we deserve and was raised from death to give us eternal life. There were many witnesses to the resurrected Christ who told firsthand their experiences of his resurrection power. Of that, there is no debate.

People find their only hope in Christ. That is why we say with confidence, "I believe in God the Father Almighty, maker of heaven and earth." It just makes sense and it fills us with hope for eternity.

Read on, for the best news lies just ahead. In the next chapter we meet the One who, having made us, gave himself up for us.

CHAPTER SIX

Who Was The Most Amazing Person Who Ever Lived?

What is the most important question you will ever answer in your life? What consequence does Jesus and his message have for this millennium? In this chapter, you will find answers to these and other questions. Read on and be encouraged and assured.

"**I** am trying here to prevent anyone saying the really foolish thing that people often say about him: 'I'm ready to accept Jesus as a great moral teacher, but I don't accept his claim to be God.' That is one thing we must not say. A man who was merely a man and said the sort of things Jesus said wouldn't be a great moral teacher. He'd be either a lunatic—on a level with a man who says he's a poached egg—or else he'd be the devil of hell. You must make your choice. Either this man was, and is, the Son of God, or else a madman or something worse." [9]

C.S. Lewis was right! Either Jesus Christ was Lord or he was a lunatic or he was a liar. He was God or the greatest idiot or the greatest con artist in history. It cannot be all or any combination of these, but it must be one of these three. A theology professor at a seminary lectured his class about the lack of certainty in what I call this "Elijah time." Before his class he bemoaned, "There is no such thing as certainty and security any more. We can know nothing for sure." A sharp new student raised his hand and asked, "Professor, do you really believe that?" "I believe it with all my heart," he responded. "I'm absolutely certain of it." He was certain of his uncertainty, secure in his insecurity. He believed in his unbelief.

"I believe in God the Father Almighty, Maker of heaven and earth and in Jesus Christ, his only Son, our Lord." There was no doubt in the minds of the framers of the Apostles' Creed about Jesus Christ.

Yet, sad to say, that professor was right about our era. We live in a time of amazing uncertainty. That is why I say our time reflects that time when Elijah challenged the people on Mount Carmel to make up their minds. An epistemological crisis has gripped the entire Western World. Epistemology is that division of philosophy that investigates the nature and origin of what we claim to know. Some people simply refuse to accept anything as truth regardless of the facts supporting it. Others hang their whole eternity on bizarre and obviously fraudulent reports as though they were gospel truth. They fall for any one of a plethora of ancient heresies that have been carefully repackaged for contemporary consumption. So, our generation slumbers in an intellectual netherworld somewhere between unhealthy cynicism and credulity. In such a setting, there is no more urgent question than this: Exactly who is Jesus Christ? What do we know about his message? Does anything he said have relevance for our generation? This chapter explores these questions and provides concrete answers to them.

THE MANY FACES OF JESUS

At a meeting of Christians I attended a few days ago, discussion centered on the *Westminster Shorter Catechism* answer about the application of the eighth commandment. The question is "What is required in the eighth commandment?" The answer the Catechism gives is "The eighth commandment requires the lawful procuring and furthering the wealth and outward estate of ourselves and others." One member of the group protested, "Not the Jesus I know!" She went on to declare with assumed authority that Jesus wanted nothing to do with the wealthy. Such is her perception of Christ and his example. I have no doubt others would hold the same or a similar viewpoint.

Just who is Jesus Christ and what does he stand for? A collage of characters portrays Jesus as we enter the twenty-first century. For some, he is seen as a political revolutionary; for others, as a friend to the paupers. Some would portray him as a peasant caught up in social upheaval, a sophisticated magician, a charismatic leader, or a hell-fire-and-brimstone prophet. Some of these patchy portraits may be more autobiographical of their proponents than authentically biblical. Sometimes the imaginary pictures we carry around of Jesus reveal far more about us than they do about him.

One famous preacher spoke eloquently to a packed-house gathering of Pittsburgh civic leaders recently and likened Jesus to the illegitimate son of a young ghetto woman. His message echoed the same kinds of allegations the Pharisees made about the birth of Jesus and betrayed his understanding not only of Scripture but also of the marriage traditions of the Middle East in Jesus' time. The number of seemingly intelligent people who applauded his message later amazed and saddened me. It reinforced my belief that these are indeed Elijah times in which people are ready to praise whatever sounds good for the moment without first checking it in Scripture. Such a description as that speaker gave may make for good political oratory but it is a long way from Biblical truth. It is flawed from start to finish. Tragically, it indicates that, while calling himself "Reverend," he apparently at some point determined he would not allow the Bible to get in the way of his message.

The Apostles' Creed authors, on the other hand, took the Bible as their final source. Their message has relevance for daily living in every generation because it is squarely biblical. What they said about Jesus was based first and last on God's word. For that reason, everything they say is of sterling quality and that is why it has withstood the onslaught of the centuries. When they professed belief in "Jesus Christ, his only Son our Lord," we need to know exactly what they had in mind. Perhaps their understanding was guided by Jesus' autobiography.

WHO DO THEY SAY THAT CHRIST IS?

Belief in a person always involves opinions about that person. It is impossible to trust a person who one finds to be untrustworthy. When we say, "I believe...in Jesus Christ," we need to first determine which of C.S. Lewis' options we will accept. In Lewis' own words, "You must make your choice. Either this man was, and is, the Son of God, or else a madman or something worse." We cannot get by saying that Jesus was a really good man or that he was an excellent teacher or great leader. As we shall see presently, he did not leave us with those alternatives. Moreover, two thousand years of the history of Christianity either stands or falls for each of us on how we answer this question. If Jesus Christ is not believable, Christianity is nothing more than a cult whose leader makes Jim Jones, David Koresh, Joseph Smith, and all the other cult leaders of the last two thousand years look like a collection of saints. Their combined impact is so tiny it disappears when put beside the influence of Jesus. If Jesus was deluded or delinquent, a holocaust far worse than Adolf Hitler's has occurred in Jesus' name. Every martyr in Christian history died painfully for no reason. What is worse, they each went out into a godless and hopeless eternity. If Jesus is a phony or a fool, even now people of good intentions are being punished for an indefensible cause. If Jesus is not the Messiah, all Christian history stands on sand. This alone should make any reasonable person, regardless of his or her own religious convictions, want to know what the framers of the Apostles' Creed were thinking when they inserted the line about believing in Jesus Christ.

The first part of the answer to that question is found in the Creed itself in the use of the word "Christ" to describe him. We have already acknowledged that the Creed is most likely not the actual work of the Apostles themselves but more likely of their first followers. It finds its roots in apostolic times and in the early church. Even though the passage of the centuries since then has caused the word "Christ" to be regarded as part of the commonly accepted name of Jesus, in the early church that was not the case. "Christ" is, in reality, not a name but a title. It is a direct derivation of the Greek word *Christos*, which means "the anointed one." The Hebrew form of "Christ" is "Messiah," which also means anointed. The Jews held this name in absolute regard to be used exclusively for the One whose coming they had been looking for across the centuries. So, when the original authors of the Creed said, "I believe...in Jesus Christ," they were, in effect, professing, "I believe that Jesus is the Messiah of God who is prophesied in the Old Testament." They had made up their minds long before C. S. Lewis challenged his readers to make up theirs. Why would they make such a bold profession in a world governed by cruel Rome and in which the Jewish leaders held such sway that they could force Rome to kill an innocent man?

WHO DOES THE BIBLE SAY CHRIST IS?

Andrew, one of the first disciples, won his brother, Simon Peter, with one of the first professions of faith recorded in the New Testament. *"We have found the Messias, which is, being interpreted, the Christ"* (John 1:41). As soon as he met Jesus, Andrew knew who he was. Similarly, the Samaritan woman at the well, whose heart had just been conquered by the living Jesus, asked her neighbors, *"Is not this the Christ?"* (John 4:29). She, too, quickly made up her mind. The Jews, on the other hand, put Jesus to death for claiming to be the Messiah.

This leads us to remember what the Old Testament says about Jesus. It immediately poses a question about whether Christianity, as outlined by the Creed, can withstand a challenge by the Old Testament prophecies. If Elijah, Isaiah, Jeremiah, Daniel, Amos, and their peers had been alive when Jesus came to Earth, would they have unanimously declared, "This man matches everything we said to describe the Messiah?" If Jesus fits their description, we are forced to conclude that the framers of the Creed were correct to assign the title Christ to him.

Pascal said, "The greatest of the proofs of Jesus Christ are the prophecies." Jesus himself used the Old Testament prophecies as proof of his true identity when, on the day of his resurrection, he met the two disciples on the Emmaus Road and declared, *"Beginning at Moses and all the prophets, he expounded unto them in all the scriptures the things concerning himself"* *(Luke 24:27)*. Was Jesus right? Or, was this just one more string of lies in a life of lies? Let us see.

Over and over again, Matthew, the Jewish tax collector who had such a passion for his own people that he intentionally wrote a gospel with the Jews in mind, affirms his conviction that Jesus is the promised Messiah. Read his gospel and see how many times he relates events in Christ's life with those told by the writers of the Old Testament. Sixteen times Matthew tells the story of Jesus and adds that an event *"fulfilled which was spoken of the Lord by the prophet"* or some similar statement.

Matthew, the Jew, understands that from beginning to end, the Old Testament is a book that looks forward to one great future event, the coming of the Messiah. Moses, writing in Genesis, predicts that the seed of a woman will finally crush the evil serpent's head (see Genesis 3:15). He uses the word for seed as it is never used again in Hebrew writings to indicate that the Messiah would be born without the input of a man. We shall see in the next chapter that Moses understood that, somehow, there would be a virgin birth.

Other prophecies are equally specific telling us, for example, that the Messiah will come from Judah's tribe and David's line and that his birthplace will be tiny Bethlehem, not, as one might expect, the capital city of Jerusalem. Not only the place, but also the time is told. It will be before the scepter finally departs from Judah and while the Second Temple still stands. A prophet with a message focused distinctly on repentance and righteousness will immediately precede him. His ministry will include such miracles as healing the sick and raising the dead. Although he is by right a king, when he finally arrives in Jerusalem he will ride the foal of an ass. He will be betrayed for thirty pieces of silver. He will be mocked and reviled as he suffers. Vinegar will be forced on him as a thirst quencher. A lot will be held to determine the division of his garments. He will be pierced. He will be buried in a rich man's grave. Although dead, he will not be left in Hades, nor will his body see corruption. Through the circulation of his gospel, many people will find righteousness. This is the Messiah's biography according to Old Testament prophecies. This is the biography of Jesus the Christ, God's only begotten son.

Imagine that someone who had never read the Bible was given only the Old Testament. That person would read these prophecies and try to imagine just whom the subject might be. Imagine, then, that someone else who never read the Bible was given only the New Testament. This person would read about the life and times of Jesus Christ and be puzzled about why someone like him endured the experiences he had. Now imagine that these two people met up one day and got into a conversation about what they had read. The first one might declare, "I read a fascinating book but somehow the end is missing. Let me tell you about it." The second would reply, "I know a similar story, but until now I did not understand its beginning." As they talked further, they would realize that between them they possessed completeness of the truth, the whole truth, and nothing but the truth, Jesus Christ, to whom all the prophets point. As one sage puts it, "The New is in the Old contained and the Old is in the New explained." Apart from Jesus Christ, the Old Testament is like an unfinished literary symphony.

WHO DOES CHRIST SAY HE IS?

The credibility of who Jesus Christ is hangs most of all on what he claims about himself. Seven times in John's gospels alone he makes specific claims about his own identity.

The Bread of Life
"I am the bread of life: he that cometh to me shall never hunger; and he that believeth on me shall never thirst...I am the living bread which came down from heaven: if any man eat of this bread, he shall live for ever: and the bread that I will give is my flesh, which I will give for the life of the world" (John 6:35,51).

The Light of the World
"I am the light of the world: he that followeth me shall not walk in darkness, but shall have the light of life...As long as I am in the world, I am the light of the world" (John 8:12; 9:5).

The Door
"I am the door of the sheep...I am the door: by me if any man enter in, he shall be saved, and shall go in and out, and find pasture" (John 10:7,9).

The Good Shepherd
"I am the good shepherd: the good shepherd giveth his life for the sheep...I am the good shepherd, and know my sheep, and am known of mine" (John 10:11,14).

The Resurrection and the Life
"I am the resurrection, and the life: he that believeth in me, though he were dead, yet shall he live" (John 11:25).

The Way, The Truth and the Life
"I am the way, the truth, and the life: no man cometh unto the Father, but by me" (John 14:6).

The True Vine

"I am the true vine, and my Father is the husbandman...I am the vine, ye are the branches: He that abideth in me, and I in him, the same bringeth forth much fruit: for without me ye can do nothing" (John 15:1,5).

During the 1990s Persian Gulf War, a group of British soldiers wandered off into the desert and, before they realized it, were lost and disoriented. They drifted aimlessly, hoping for some kind of indicator that would help them know their whereabouts and find their way back to their encampment. After a long time, they encountered a five-star American general on a surveillance mission. Without explaining their circumstances, the lost and disoriented servicemen asked, "Do you have any idea where we are?" Their form of address demonstrated no understanding of this general's superiority. There was no salute, and they looked unkempt and disordered. Noting this seeming lack of respect for rank, the general indignantly asked, "Before I answer, do you have any idea who I am?" "Oh, wonderful," exclaimed one of the soldiers to his buddies, "we don't have a clue where we are and he doesn't even know who he is!"

That can never be said of Jesus! He claims all these titles for himself without apology. He says he is bread that feeds for now and forever, light for the world, the door to salvation, the only truly good shepherd, the giver of eternal life, the indispensable vine, and the only way to God the Father. What is more, in the Greek text Jesus uses an emphatic personal pronoun that affirms both his deity and his absolute eternal sovereignty. That pronoun is *eimi* for *"I am."* It is a way of saying, *"I and I alone am these things."*

Does that sound familiar? It should. *Eime* is the Greek equivalent of the Hebrew name God chose for himself when Moses asked for an identity to strengthen his authority before the Pharaoh and the enslaved children of Israel in Exodus 3:14. God called himself "I AM." It was his official name that described his unchanging character and eternal power. Jesus declares through each of these *"I am"* statements in John's gospel absolute parity with the God of Moses.

WHO DO YOU SAY JESUS IS?

"When Jesus came into the coasts of Caesarea Philippi, he asked his disciples, saying, 'Whom do men say that I the Son of man am?' And they said, 'Some say that thou art John the Baptist: some, Elias; and others, Jeremias, or one of the prophets.' He saith unto them, 'But whom say ye that I am?'" (Matthew 16:13-16).

There was no personal identity crisis with Jesus Christ. He understood beyond any shadow of a doubt who he was. Do you know who he is? When you profess "I believe," who is he for you? Perhaps you have watched the movie version of *Ben Hur* on television, but did you know this story behind it? Robert Ingersoll was a seemingly brilliant scholar and an avowed atheist. One day he was engaged in conversation with Lew Wallace, the *Ben Hur* author, who also professed atheism. Ingersoll declared, "Lew, I frankly believe that for you to give credibility to Jesus Christ in a story like this is an affront to honest scholarship. I wish you would reconsider what you have done." Wallace said, "I will read the New Testament for myself and add a chapter discrediting Jesus Christ." He assumed he was committing himself to a simple one- or two-night reading-and-writing assignment. Instead, a spirit of inquisitiveness entered Lew Wallace. With the eye of a determined critic, he ended up poring over the pages of the New Testament for six years. When he was finished, Lew Wallace went to his friend Ingersoll and said, "I told you I would write a chapter discrediting Jesus Christ. Instead I have come to the absolute conviction that he is the Jewish Messiah, the Savior of the world, and I have taken him as my personal Redeemer."

Jesus still asks of every man and woman who come near him his question. As you read these words, he is asking you, *"Whom say ye that I am?"* It is the most important question you will ever answer. How do you answer? Is he the biggest liar who ever lived? The craziest lunatic? Or, the Lord of your life? Remember, only one of these answers fits and there are no other options. *"What think ye of Christ? Whose son is he?"* *(Matthew 22:42).* This is the most important answer you will ever give in your life. Answer it clearly for your whole eternity hangs in the balance.

What does who Christ is mean for us today? If we are already Christians, believers in the Lord Jesus, it means that we have a faith that stands on impregnable grounds. It means that when we attend church to worship, or when we kneel alone to pray for ourselves and those we love, or when, in the day that sadness comes to us and we ask his help and comfort, or when our hearts are heavy because of sin and personal failure, that this Jesus Christ, Eternal Son of God Almighty, hears, heeds, and gives us deliverance and comfort. To believe in him means to believe in the things he stood for and died for. To believe in him is to commit our lives to the highest goals and ideals possible. It means to commit our lives to God and his work in the world. It means to know that we have everlasting life in heaven. Can you say and will you say, "I believe in Jesus Christ His Only Son, Our Lord"? When we can say this and mean it, we have said everything we need to say for a secure eternity because *"If thou shalt confess with thy mouth the Lord Jesus, and shalt believe in thine heart that God hath raised him from the dead, thou shalt be saved" (Romans 10:9).*

Read on and discover two sides of one of the most intriguing mysteries the world has ever faced.

CHAPTER SEVEN

Where Did Jesus Christ Come From?

Is your birth a mystery? Are you a miracle baby? You may be and not even know it. In this chapter we're going to explore the first side of one of the greatest mysteries in all history. We're also going to see what it takes to make sense out of a miracle and what a difference believing in miracles makes to all of life.

SAY HELLO TO DOLLY

Dolly made headlines all over the world a few years ago as the most unusual sheep that ever was. Does that sound strange? Only if you do not know that Dolly is a first-in-her-class kind of animal, and we're not talking about agricultural shows. No, Dolly is first in her class because she was the product of a cloning experiment. Her birth was hailed across the globe as a mark of how far we have come in our understanding of genetic principles. Some news headlines even called Dolly's birth a miracle. In this chapter and the next one, we are going to be thinking about the greatest miracle the world has ever seen.

THE SECURITY OF UNCERTAINTY

A Christian businessman told me about a seminary board meeting where business leaders and theologians met to compose a mission statement for a new seminary project. He said he concluded that business leaders often demonstrate a higher level of commitment to their Christian beliefs than some clergy types. Some of the theologians crafted sentences that spun on weasel words and phrases that would make a Washington, D.C., spinmeister proud. When pressed, they acknowledged that they were looking for a statement that was inoffensive to potential donors to the project. Finally, one frustrated business leader declared, "If raising money is what we are about, let's just say that. In any case, we should say what we mean and say it so that nobody will have any doubt what we are really trying to do."

The Apostles' Creed authors never resorted to semantic gymnastics, those loop-de-loop words and phrases specifically designed to change from circumstance to circumstance. The Creed authors had one primary goal in mind: They would give Christians a plain fact statement that would summarize the primary principles of their faith and would direct their lives in good ways.

LIFE LINES

What we believe determines how we think. How we think in turn determines how we live. For this reason, it is vitally important to know what we believe and to know why we believe it. That is the reason for this book, and it is never any truer than when we come to the Creed's statement "I believe in...Jesus Christ His only Son our Lord, who was conceived by the Holy Spirit." Only a fool would deny belief in Jesus Christ. There is too much historic evidence to refute his existence. It is not that we believe in Jesus that makes us Christians. It is what we believe about him that separates us from the rest of the world.

BELIEVING VERSUS UNDERSTANDING

"Joseph, thou son of David, fear not to take unto thee Mary thy wife: for that which is conceived in her is of the Holy Ghost" (Matthew 1:20).

Ever since part of my undergraduate training in psychology required me to conduct an experiment with fruit flies, the study of genetics has fascinated me. As part of my course assignment, I established an environment in which a brown-eyed fruit fly was mated with a green-eyed fruit fly. The study was intended to confirm that approximately half of those two fruit flies' descendents would have two brown eyes and the other half would have two green eyes. None of them would have a brown eye on one side of their head and a green eye on the other side. Nor would any of them have an eye color other than brown and green. The result was both controllable and predictable. That is part of what I find intriguing about the science of genetics and science in particular. I like controllability and predictability. I also like to know that the world is a very ordered place. It is not nearly as chance oriented as some people might think.

THE UNCONTROLLABLE AND THE UNPREDICTABLE

Yet, there are some things about life that fly in the face of this orderliness. I could never convince you of the truth of those things through the use of scientific principles. For example, using scientific principles, I could never prove for you that Jesus was not Joseph's natural child. Only Mary or Joseph and God can prove that. Mary and Joseph perhaps told Matthew and Luke, and the Holy Spirit witnessed to Matthew and Luke that it was so. Matthew and Luke then passed this truth along to us.

There are many other truths that I could never help you understand. A few years ago a Hubble space telescope showed that the rings around Saturn travel at a very rapid speed in opposite directions. That is easy for me to believe. Every day I travel Interstate 279 to and from downtown Pittsburgh, and traffic on that part of America's interstate system travels at a very high rate of speed in opposite directions, also. However, that Hubble telescope then showed that those opposite-directions-fast-traveling Saturn rings run in the same tracks without ever colliding. How can that be? It defies my imagination. I cannot explain it. It simply is. Why don't Saturn's rings crash? When cars on I-279 travel in opposite directions on the same side of the freeway, the result is always a mess. Police, paramedics, and fire trucks are called to help clean up the wreckage. Now if we could do it here the way it happens around Saturn, think of the money we could save on highway construction! We would need only one side on every highway. I cannot explain how Saturn's rings do not collide. Nevertheless, it is true!

How does e-mail work? I don't understand that either. I could never explain it to you. Yet, I use it every day. All I know is that when I send out a message it gets to the right person—even on the other side of the world—at about the speed of light. I cannot explain that, but I know it is. So, I believe in it.

How does a bumblebee fly? I'm told that bumblebees are not supposed to be able to fly because they are not aeronautically correct in their design. I guess bumblebees do not study the principles of aeronautics, so they fly even though the best minds in that branch of science cannot figure out how. I do not understand but I believe.

In a similar way, my great-great-grandfather never dreamed that one day people on opposite sides of the ocean could converse by telephone, or that hot water would run into a bathtub at the turn of a tap, or that jet airplanes would travel to America in about as many hours as the best ships in his time took in days to get there. Nor did yours, I expect.

I still get a chuckle every time I think about Lawrence of Arabia's entourage taking the water taps from their Paris hotel bathrooms after the 1919 Paris peace talks. Those men of the desert figured that if they could just connect those magic taps to the walls of their palaces and tents, there would be no more desert droughts! How did those taps work? Simple, you say and you begin to explain the intricacies of indoor plumbing. For Lawrence's compatriots, however, running water was not part of their experience. They could not understand it, so they took it at face value and decided it was something inside the tap that made water run. It made sense to take the hotel taps instead of the towels. Some things are real and true and wonderful even though they defy explanation.

Think about electricity! We do not understand it but we believe in it because we use it. I remember when electricity was installed in my grandmother's home for the first time. It so fascinated her that she repeatedly flicked the wall switch (as I write these words, I can still hear the "thunk" sound of that switch) and marveled that the light turned on and off at her command each time. She did not understand what electricity is any more than we do, but that did not stop her from believing in it and benefiting from it.

Or, consider the miracle of life, perhaps your own life. Explain how sperm and egg somehow unite and become a person without the direct intervention of supernatural power. You cannot do it. A biologist at a leading mid-western university was able, a few years ago, to replicate an oat seed so similar in every way to the real thing that none of the hundreds of students and professors who saw it could discern the difference with absolute certainty. Finally, the biologist said, "The only way to tell the difference is to plant both seeds in soil. When we do that, only one will come to life for the other has no inherent life power." The wise scientist knew that it is possible to replicate only the seed's physical characteristics but the Holy Spirit alone can create life, the same Spirit that brought life to Mary's untouched womb. There is no life, either physical or spiritual, where God's Spirit is not involved. Life is created only through the Lord of life! *"Thou sendest forth thy spirit, they are created: and thou renewest the face of the earth" (Psalm 104:30).*

LIMITED EAGLES

On my first visit to the Belfast zoo as a youngster, everything I saw impressed me. The thing that awed me most on that visit was seeing an eagle for the first time. The magnificent bird was everything I had imagined and more. I recall that it was housed in a cage with a roof about twenty feet high. I've since thought many times what a hindrance that was to the eagle's potential. That splendid creature spent its life handicapped because he could never soar as eagles are made to do. In the same way, people who believe only what can be proved spend their lives in a cage that hampers their imaginations. They miss God's true intentions for them. Perhaps that is why no atheist has ever contributed a good and lasting discovery that benefited humanity's cause. Harnessed by the self-imposed limits of their reasoning skills, they spend their lives mentally caged and their potential never is achieved. *"But they that wait upon the LORD shall renew their strength; they shall mount up with wings as eagles" (Isaiah 40:31).* The word for *"wait"* means to contemplate what God can do.

To live truly fulfilled lives, we need a God who is bigger than us and who can achieve greater and more wonderful things than we can comprehend, without him. I need a God who understands and controls some things I cannot comprehend. Don't you? It takes faith to break through the mental bars of our limited imaginations. That faith, the Bible says, is God's gift to us. He gives it to all who ask him for it.

"He was conceived by the Holy Spirit." That is a faith statement because it cannot be proved in this world. I believe this *Life Line* with all my heart, even though I could not demonstrate it for you if my life depended on doing that. Only God comprehends how Christ's conception was accomplished. Somehow the Father on high joined himself to Mary, and his Son, Jesus Christ our Lord, became a man. We believe that because we believe in a God for whom nothing is impossible. He makes the miraculous look effortless. Moreover, Christians believe in God's Son, Jesus Christ, and we know at the core of our being that he was no ordinary man. Therefore, no ordinary conception could have produced him.

Did you catch the order of that statement? We do not believe in Jesus because of his conception. We believe in his conception because we believe in him. The "how" of his conception is no problem when you know the "whom" of it. There is nothing God is not able to bring about. With him, the impossible is imminently possible.

Just as a magnifying glass brings out the splendid inner beauty of a rose, so Jesus Christ makes God plainer for the eyes of our heart. Jesus is not merely like God. He is God. Jesus does not simply show us what God is like. He shows us who God is. He possesses all the qualities God possesses. God, who is a "Spirit, infinite, eternal and unchangeable in being wisdom, power, justice, holiness, goodness and truth,"[10] took on flesh and bones in Jesus.

A Jehovah Witness stood up in a church service one evening and challenged a godly preacher on this subject: "How can you claim that Jesus Christ is co-equal with the eternal Father? That can never be true for no son is ever as old as his father." The detractor smugly assumed that he had won the argument with that one statement. Instead, the minister looked the cultist in the eye and asked him, "What did you just call God?" The detractor said, "I called him, 'eternal Father.'" "I thought so," replied the minister. "Surely the only way to be the eternal Father is to have an eternal Son. If the Son did not always exist with the Father, then God is not eternally a Father but only latterly so." The cultist was speechless. He had no comeback.

THE DIFFERENCE IT MAKES

What difference does it make that we believe the Holy Spirit conceived Jesus Christ? It makes an amazing difference. It first gives us a better sense of how big God is. Accepting the fact of Christ's unique conception changes our whole outlook on life. Miracles are not a problem for us because when God can fertilize a virgin's egg, he can do whatever he decides to do in other situations also. He can work miracles and bring about circumstances in our lives that defy the accepted boundaries we think we understand. Too many people in the church and our society have a concept of God that is stunted by man-made standards. Like the zoo eagle I wrote about earlier, a cage limits them, too. Like the eagle, their spirits are imprisoned.

I believe in miracles because I am one. My life has been transformed by a power that is greater than all the human power the world could ever muster. It takes a miracle to make a believing Christian out of an insecure little boy. It takes a miracle to effectively transmit the saving power of Calvary's cross across almost two millennia to sinners living in this generation. If you are a Christian, you are a walking miracle. That is something worth celebrating and telling at every opportunity. God has moved beyond all the known rules of human minds and achieved something wonderful in your life.

WHEN KNOWING IS ENOUGH

Believing in the Holy Spirit's power to conceive a child in a virgin's womb is also a source of comfort, confidence, and courage for us. One of the oldest and finest ancient catechisms of Reformed Christianity asks the question, "What is your only comfort in life and death?" The answer begins, "That I with body and soul, both in life and death, am not my own, but belong unto my faithful Savior Jesus Christ."[11] There is our comfort. It is that the same Spirit of Jesus Christ never leaves nor forsakes us. Those of us who believe in him know that we are never alone. Thus we do not fear for he accompanies us through all of life and even in death. *"For whether we live, we live unto the Lord; and whether we die, we die unto the Lord: whether we live therefore, or die, we are the*

Lord's" (Romans 14:8). He leads us, guides us, and protects us from eternal harm.

Some years ago, Elisabeth Elliot stayed overnight at our home in Pascagoula, Mississippi. That evening she spoke eloquently of her experience when news first reached her that the Ecuador Aucas had murdered her husband, Jim. She bore witness to the comfort God brought her even in the face of that awful tragedy. So Christ also promises to comfort, with supernatural comfort, each of us who trust him no matter what life brings us.

Not only do we find comfort in believing in this big God who can use a virgin to birth his Son, we also find confidence in believing in him. Our confidence comes from knowing God is in charge of the universe and that he leaves no loose threads as he knits history together. Recently, Barbara and I walked along a familiar coastal pathway near Bangor, County Down. It was a stormy night and we normally would not have been out except that we had just been called home to Northern Ireland following the death of Barbara's mother only eight days after the unexpected death of Barbara's brother, David. We needed some time alone together. For that reason, we walked in spite of the weather. As we walked together, the ferocious Irish Sea crashed on the rocks beside us. Looking out across the water we saw a ship that was headed toward Belfast docks. "How will it ever make it?" I asked myself. The wild waves played their cruel game mercilessly all around it. Yet, it scarcely moved. We soon realized that something we could not see at first held the ship steady. That vessel was attached by a long chain that broke down through the cruel waves and anchored it to the rocks at the bottom of the sea. In a similar way, when we believe in God's ability to effect a supernatural conception, we know that we have an anchor that will hold us steady when life's storms assail us. Knowing we have an anchor fastened to the Rock of Ages brings a supernatural confidence that nothing in the world can ever undermine.

Finally, because we believe in the power of the Holy Spirit to bring about supernatural events, we have a courage that is not natural. In the days following the sudden collapse of the Berlin Wall, the world learned that even sixty years of official Communist repression could not stifle the followers of Jesus Christ on the other side of the Iron Curtain. The courage and devotion of ordinary men and women, filled with Holy Spirit power, enabled them to practice their faith courageously in defiance of the worst that hostile rulers could direct their way. It was a testimony unmatched since the days of the Roman Empire. That courage comes from knowing we have a God who will never be defeated by any humanly devised plans or limits. That same courage, demonstrated in the lives of thousands of Christians in the former Soviet Union, is available to all Christians. For about two thousand years now it has enabled millions of individual Christians to rise up and overcome circumstances others deemed impossible.

These are just a few illustrations of the difference that believing in Christ's conception by the Holy Spirit makes in our lives. Belief, sometimes called "faith," in supernatural events like Christ's miraculous conception leads us to experience life on a higher plane than is otherwise possible. It causes us to rise above our natural abilities and become more than we can be without faith in God's supernatural power.

"I believe—Jesus Christ was conceived by the Holy Spirit." Because I believe that, I live life with the expectation that God will keep surprising me in ways I have not yet imagined. Thus, my prayers are neither hindered nor limited.

This is the first side of one of life's great mysteries, an event that staggers the brightest minds in human history. Yet, when we speak of it we are speaking of something that is incomplete for it is only the first half of the story. In chapter eight we will explore the second half. More good news about what believing in God's supernatural power can do lies ahead. Read on. More wonderful news lies just ahead.

Can a Virgin Have a Baby?

If you possessed only one side of perhaps the most fascinating mystery in history, what could you do with it? Probably nothing, except be really frustrated because you were missing the rest of the story. It would be like owning half the pieces of a jigsaw puzzle. The Apostles' Creed authors do not leave us in that predicament. Instead, they give us both pieces of the puzzle, presenting the other side of the mystery to us. In this chapter we will explore the other side of the story and talk about how God did it. Read on and let your mind grow.

LARRY KING'S BIG QUESTION

CNN talk show host Larry King prides himself in being first among all the news show hosts to secure great interviews. His subjects run the gamut all the way from world leaders to Madonna—the singer, that is. Presidents, peacemakers, Hollywood's latest stars, and war heroes all find a platform on Larry King's nightly television show. Presidential wannabees announce their candidacies before King's viewers, while others confess their dirty laundry or try to make recompense for their wrongs. Others promote their latest books or movies. Larry King, a professed Jew, makes no bones about his first fascination. Religious themes are especially intriguing for him. My guess is that he is a man in search of himself. He has interviewed the leaders of almost all the world's best-known religions and even had them debate one another about their beliefs. Had CNN and *Larry King Live* been on the air around the middle of the second century A.D. when the Creed was composed, my guess is Larry King would have invited the authors of the Apostles' Creed to appear with him and would have asked them some pointed questions. Not long ago a newspaper reporter asked Larry King a carte blanche question, "If you could interview anyone in world history, who would it be?" Without a blink, Larry King, the Jew, smiled back and said, "Jesus Christ. He is in a class by himself, by far the most intriguing person who ever lived." "What would you ask him?" the reporter continued. With intensity, Larry King immediately replied, "Were you really born of a virgin? If he said 'yes,' that would change everything about the world."

Larry King is right! It does change everything about the world, even for those who neither know it nor believe it. The virgin birth of Jesus Christ, the other side of the mystery of how God became a man, changes all of life.

THE DAWN'S EARLY LIGHT

"Jesus Christ…was conceived by the Holy Spirit and born of the Virgin Mary." These two *Life Lines* come one on top of the other like two primary parts of a puzzle. Humanity's first dawn became a cloud-covered day the moment Adam sinned. Perfection was ruined for all time. Never mind that my mother thought it was preserved until after I was born and maybe yours thought the same about you. The fact is that nothing could ever be really right again. *"By one man sin entered into the world, and death by sin; and so death passed upon all men, for that all have sinned" (Romans 5:12).*

Just when it looked like everything was ruined, God punched a hole in the darkness. A virgin's child will solve this man-made predicament. God said: *"I will put enmity between thee and the woman, and between thy seed and her seed; it shall bruise thy head, and thou shalt bruise his heel" (Genesis 3:15).*

The words *"her seed"* contain an amazing declaration of how the Messiah's birth would happen. What a difference a word makes! The word *"seed"* (Hebrew, *zera*) is used more than one hundred times in the Bible and, except for this one time, it is always in reference to the male of the species. Nowhere else is *zera* used in connection with the female. God through the Bible writers was revealing a life-giving principle thousands of years before science would prove it. Today, because of sophisticated methods of biological research, we can say for sure that the procreative seed is always resident in the male. Ask any biologist. The only exception in all human history is this one.

Why should it be? The answer is only found in Jesus Christ. He was not born as a result of a union between a woman and a man. He was fathered by the Holy Spirit and born of a woman. No wonder Larry King wants to interview him! The wonderful news is that in the Bible, Christ has enabled his Spirit to reveal answers to many of the questions we might want to ask of him. The Jewish prophet Isaiah, for example, says his birth would be a signal day for Israel: *"The Lord himself shall give you a sign; Behold, a virgin shall conceive, and bear a son, and shall call his name Immanuel" (Isaiah 7:14).* Matthew, the Jewish evangelist for Jesus, writes it this way: *"The angel of the Lord appeared unto him in a dream, saying, 'Joseph, thou son of David, fear not to take unto thee Mary thy wife: for that which is conceived in her is of the Holy Ghost.' ...All this was done, that it might be fulfilled which was spoken of the Lord by the prophet, saying, 'Behold, a virgin shall be with child, and shall bring forth a son, and they shall call his name Emmanuel, which being interpreted is, God with us'" (Matthew 1:20-23).* Paul, a Hebrew of the Hebrews, a legal scholar with few equals, writes it to the Galatians: *"When the fulness of the time was come, God sent forth his Son, made of a woman, made under the law" (Galatians 4:4).* Notice how again and again they repeat the amazing significance of a child born of a woman instead of following the traditional Hebrew pattern of relating a child to its father.

MARY'S MARVEL

"My soul doth magnify the Lord, And my spirit hath rejoiced in God my Saviour" (Luke 1:46,47). One of the initially important books in my spiritual growth as a new Christian was J.B. Phillips' *Your God is Too Small.* Having somehow grown up with a narrowly defined view of God in my imagination for years, Dr. Phillips' little book broadened the horizons of my understanding and broke down the fences of my prejudices. He showed me that God is a lot bigger than I could imagine. When the angel told Mary she was about to bear a child while still a virgin, she did not, so far as we know from Scripture, question what God was about. She did not, like Jonah, try to run a different way to avoid what God had in mind. Nor did she, like Abraham, try to help God out somehow. She simply responded, in effect, "My mind now explodes with a new sense of how big God is!" Can you imagine how her limited understanding of life was distended by that encounter with a heavenly messenger?

THE SHRIVELING SAVIOR

This book began by talking about Elijah's generation and its concept of God. For King Ahab and most of his citizens, the perception was that

God was not large enough to satisfy their needs. As a result, they aligned Jehovah with the Baals and created a concoction that had streaks of many deities. It gave the same credence to the gods with a small g as it did to the large G, Jehovah God.

We do the same thing in different ways. The new age combines the perceived strengths of a plethora of deities because it has concluded somehow that the God of the Bible is insufficient for these times.

Is your God too small? Is he a shriveled savior? How easy it can be to define God according to our particular experience and pre-defined expression of him. It does not help to profess that Jesus Christ was conceived by God's Spirit and born of a virgin mother if you don't think God is big enough to help you where you need him the most. The question of God's size lies at the back of every doubt.

It was behind Abraham's adulterous relationship with Hagar; Moses' temper; David's escapade with Bathsheba and her husband, Uriah; Judas' betrayal of Jesus for thirty pieces of silver; Peter's denial; and Paul's manhunt for the first Christians. Each lost sight of God's bigness and each unintentionally, yet effectively, created a small g god in his own restricted imagination.

HELPING GOD CARRY THE LOAD

We do the same thing. Worry, for example, is evidence that we worship a god too small. The level of worry in my heart is a measure of the size of my God. The worrier gets anxious because he is fearful that God will not be there or will not be big enough when the tough times come. His God is too small. An elderly woman, greatly worried about her troubles, both real and imagined, exasperated her children and grandchildren. Finally, a favorite grandson declared, "Granny, we've done just about everything there is to settle your mind and it hasn't helped, so let's just give your troubles over to the Lord." A startled look possessed the old soul's face and her lips quivered as she said, "Oh dear, has it finally come to that?" She did not understand that "that" is where it needed to be all along. Her god was of the small g variety, a deity who needed the assistance of her worry. The truth, not just for Granny but for all of us, is that it always comes to that, so we might as well begin there by bringing every care to God. If he is big enough to save us, he had better be big enough to handle our day-to-day concerns, too. Granny was up against no weak-kneed enemy, for worry is no wimp. Medical research indicates that worry and the illnesses it produces probably occupy more hospital beds than any other thing.

How can we handle our worries effectively? By giving them over to God. *"They that wait upon the LORD shall renew their strength; they shall mount up with wings as eagles; they shall run, and not be weary; and they shall walk, and not faint" (Isaiah 40:31).* Let me suggest this prescription for worry based on this verse: First, cultivate an awareness of God's size. See him as the Lord of all creation. Second, meditate on his promises. He says he will always take care of his children. Third, create an awareness of his presence. He says he will always stay with us and never leave us. Consciously imagine him with you all the time for that is where he is. Fourth, talk through your problems with him. Fifth, surrender them in trust. Believe his promise: *"Casting all your care upon him; for he careth for you"(1 Peter 5:7).*

When Jesus speaks about worry in Matthew 6:25-34, he says we can trust God for all of life's essentials. He does not say we are to sit back and do nothing, but that we are to accept whatever opportunities we encounter as God's way of providing for us in the face of our needs.

A MERCILESS MASTER

Guilt, too, is the result of a god too small! A man stood at a busy intersection in one of America's big cities during rush hour. As people hurried by, he pointed at them and declared, "Guilty!" Some people who heard him turned red with embarrassment and scurried on by, stopping to look back only after they had traveled some distance past the accuser. One woman to whom he spoke was overheard to exclaim to her friend, "How does he know?" It was her confession that she was carrying guilt about something. Probably no pain is more scarring to our souls than the pain of remorse. If worry is paying interest on tomorrow's debts, guilt is paying interest on yesterday's sins. It is the biggest thief we can know for it steals the joy God would have us all experience in his world. "Man's chief end is to glorify God, and to enjoy him forever." [12]

We all have reason to feel guilty because everybody falls short of God's intention for us. Yet, guilt is the most useless of all our emotions because it never solves anything. The great news of the gospel is that in grace Christ took all our guilt upon himself at Calvary. Because of the sacrifice he made there, our guilt is eradicated. His death was sufficient for all our sins. *"If we confess our sins, he is faithful and just to forgive us our sins, and to cleanse us from all unrighteousness" (1 John 1:9).* Notice what John declares here. He says God is *"faithful."* To be faithful means to be consistent. It means there are no exceptions. God does not forgive just some of our sins, nor does he just forgive all the sins of some people. Instead, he forgives *all* the sins of *all* the people who confess. *"All unrighteousness!"* For this reason, to confess our sins and still feel guilty about them is to have a too-small god. More than that, it is blaspheming the true God by minimizing the power of the cross to forgive us. It is to

69

whisper to God, "The cross was insufficient!" It is to demand a ransom higher than God paid when he gave up Jesus. It is to live under the terror of a master with no mercy.

When our past mistakes and personal failures are not confessed, they tend to grow inside our imagination. They become exaggerated and eventually affect our whole perspective on life. We begin to see God only as a judge who is out to get us and not as a gracious and forgiving Father whose heart's desire is to win us. The former was a view of God that occupied my imagination until I applied the message of grace to my own life. A sense of unworthiness and hopelessness crippled my joy. Perhaps that is your case, too. If so, the solution to your guilt is a relatively simple one. All you need do is acknowledge your guilt before God and ask him to help you not do that wrong again. Immediately your wrongs will be taken away. You will be free no matter what you have done. There is no sin so large that Christ's blood did not cover it all. He is big enough to cover all our sins.

Not only in failing to accept forgiveness, but also in failing to grant it, do we pay homage to the small g gods. In his book *Lee: The Last Years*, Charles Bracelen Flood reports that after the Civil War, Robert E. Lee visited a Kentucky lady who took him to the remains of a once-grand old tree in front of her house. There she wept bitterly and complained that its limbs and trunk had been destroyed by Federal artillery fire. She looked to General Lee for a word condemning the North or at least sympathizing with her loss. After a brief silence, the General said, "Cut it down, my dear Madam, and forget it." It is better to forgive the injustices of the past than to allow them to remain, lest bitterness take root and poison the rest of our life.[13] General Lee had the wisdom to know that to withhold forgiveness is to keep oneself in a cruel kind of self-imposed bondage. More than that, he had the grace to demonstrate forgiveness in his own life. To do otherwise is to create for oneself the role of demigod.

THE SMALL G GODS IN THE PUBLIC ARENA

It is not only in our personal lives that the small g gods appear. They have a way of getting themselves into public and political life as well. Sometimes their names are invoked as though riding a Democratic donkey. Sometimes they are hoisted verbally onto a Republican elephant. The thinking in each case is erroneous because the truth is that God is not aligned with any humanly devised political party. Do not look for Christ on either donkey or elephant but on a glowing white stallion (see Revelation 19:11). When we attempt to align Christ with one political position over another, Donald W. McCullough says we create a dangerous illusion of a manageable deity.[14] The God of the Creed, however, is too smart and too powerful to submit to human managers. What is more, we should know that such political rhetoric is neither original nor true. I recall well the first time I saw a Nazi storm trooper's belt. A classmate brought it to a school show-and-tell when we were about ten years old. I recall asking our teacher what the engraving on the buckle said. "Gott Mit Uns," he replied reading the German. Then he added, "It means, 'God with us.'" He paused before continuing, "The problem was they thought God was on their side, but they never stopped to ask if they were on his side!"

All these small g gods of our political imaginations are nothing more than idols like those worshiped by the followers of the Baals. They illustrate that we, too, somehow imagine we can persuade him to join our side. Not only are they impotent when it comes to meeting our needs, to follow them is an insult to the true God. Such deities can do nothing to redeem us from sin or direct our future. Moreover, they are certainly not capable of bringing about a baby from the womb of a virgin. How far better it would be if we would align our lives with him.

The God of the Bible is limitless. What is more, he operates at levels we cannot understand. *"For my thoughts are not your thoughts, neither are your ways my ways, saith the LORD. For as the heavens are higher than the earth, so are my ways higher than your ways, and my thoughts than your thoughts" (Isaiah 55:8,9).* It is impossible for us to fully comprehend the goings-on of God's mind. He is the only authentic independent, while at the same time a majority of one. His knowledge, wisdom, and reasoning powers are far greater than ours. When we try to make this limitless God conform to the small mold of our limited thinking, we always end up shortchanged and frustrated.

THE VIRGIN BIRTH OF GOD'S SON

So, what does all this have to do with the virgin birth? Simply this: It takes a God who works beyond the silly fences we erect in our minds to create a child with no earthly father. When we focus on the name and character of the One who made the plans for our redemption instead of the method of how it came about, we find that accepting the virgin birth of Jesus is not nearly so difficult. In short, when we begin to think more like Mary learned to think after her first encounter with the angel, we will find that God is able to accomplish more in and through us as well.

We need a God like Mary's God, one who is able to perform in ways that defy human imagination. When we meet this God in Jesus Christ we, too, can say with authenticity, "I believe…Jesus Christ, God's only Son, our Lord, was born of the Virgin Mary." Only when we can know this can we truly know that this same God can rekindle vanquished love, heal broken relationships, turn obstacles into opportunities and scars into healing and hope.

SINNERS UNANIMOUS

Finally, we need a Savior born of a woman who has never been sexually involved with a man because no naturally born person can save us. Ordinary people cannot save themselves, much less save someone else. If Jesus were not born of a virgin, he would be an ordinary man. If he were, as the song in *Jesus Christ Superstar* proclaims, "just a man," he would have the same problems we have. With us, he is in a hopelessly irresolvable predicament. It is that *"all have sinned, and come short of the glory of God" (Romans 3:23)* and *"the wages of sin is death" (Romans 6:23)*.

There is a unanimity about these two verses. It is that sin has infected the life of every human being ever born and has separated us all from God forever, and that sin's wages are stated without room for any exceptions. Humanly we may reason that some sins are bigger than others because under our humanly devised systems of jurisprudence, their legal consequences are far greater. We tend to classify sins by category as big and small. Murder seems bigger than anger. We tend to minimize anger and maximize murder and say that murderers deserve a harsher sentence than people who lose their tempers. Or, we reason that rape is a larger sin than lusting over a *Playboy* magazine picture. So, we minimize lust and maximize rape. In God's economy of thinking, these gradations do not exist. The Bible says that any sin creates a chasm between God and us.

How do we bridge this chasm our sin has created? We might reason that we can reach across it in our own strength if only we can live a sinless life from now until we die. The problem with that is that we have already sinned. That is why the man who stood at that city intersection saying, "Guilty," received the response he did. Each time he leveled that accusation it was correct.

ALL IN THE FAMILY

Perhaps we reason one step further. We imagine that we could have saved ourselves from sin's penalty if we could have lived a sinless life from the first breath of our birth until the moment we die. Once again, however, we have a problem. It is that since our father's sins are added to ours, our fathers would have needed to live sinless lives as well. They, however, faced a similar predicament since God says, *"I the LORD thy God am a jealous God, visiting the iniquity of the fathers upon the children unto the third and fourth generation" (Exodus 20:5).*

MONOGENES!

How, then, do we solve this universal human dilemma? There is only one way. *"If by one man's offence death reigned by one; much more they which receive abundance of grace and of the gift of righteousness shall reign in life by one, Jesus Christ" (Romans 5:17).* God's remedy was a Son, Jesus Christ, with no sinful human father. *"God hath made him to be sin for us, who knew no sin; that we might be made the righteousness of God in him" (2 Corinthians 5:21).* On the cross, God's only sinless Son took all our sin upon himself and gave us a new opportunity for eternal life in heaven. As we have already seen from St. Paul's letter to the Romans, sin's wage is death. By God's grace, the apostle does not stop there. Instead, he goes on and tells us that even though *"the wages of sin is death; but the gift of God is eternal life through Jesus Christ our Lord" (Romans 6:23).* Only a God who can work beyond the boundaries of science and human imagination can bring about such a marvelous event. He did it through the virgin birth!

Larry King is right! If Jesus Christ is born of a virgin, something wonderful has happened. In the Greek New Testament, John sees that "something" clearly: *"The Word was made flesh, and dwelt among us, (and we beheld his glory, the glory as of the only begotten of the Father)" (John 1:14).* Almost two thousand years before James Watson and Francis Crick received the 1962 Nobel prize in science for discovering the DNA molecular structure, John compounded two Greek words that formulated a new Greek word *monogenes.* The English translation of *monogenes* is *"the only begotten."* In reality, it brings the Greek word *mono,* meaning *sole, only, no other,* together with the Greek word *genes,* the root of *genetic, generation.* Watson and Crick discovered that every person ever born has two sets of genes, one set from each parent. Once in all history, a child was born with *monogenes,* or one set of genes. He was Jesus Christ, God's *"only begotten."* The genes he carried were the genes of *"The Father."* He was born of a virgin for our sakes.

Jesus Christ is the most unique person ever born. There was, however, at least one other time in history that God temporarily raised another person up for a special purpose. He is a key player in the next chapter. Read on and meet him.

CHAPTER NINE

Who Is This Man Like Me?

Which person in the Bible is more like me than any other? Which one is my representative among Christ's persecutors? Come and meet one of the most notable common men who ever lived. He is a man who made a choice that marked his soul for all eternity. Yours too! Learn from his decisions about the importance of choosing well and see the implications of his life on yours.

PONTIUS PILATE

A Sunday school youngster drew a Christmas picture for her teacher. It was an airplane with four faces peering through four windows. "What is your picture about, Hannah?" the teacher asked. "It's about the flight into Egypt," chirped up five-year-old Hannah. The teacher smiled and knew she had to do a better job of describing that part of the Christmas story. "And, who are the four people looking out the windows of the airplane, sweetie?" the teacher asked. "That's Mary, Joseph, the baby Jesus, and Pontius the pilot!" said Hannah, confident she had portrayed the story well.

Was there ever another person like Pontius Pilate, the Roman governor of Judea? He bursts onto the scene of human history for only an instant and makes a decision that consigns him to infamy for all time. He wears the white toga bordered in purple that sets him apart as a leader from Rome and is surrounded by a detail of soldiers in burnished breastplates and long-plumed helmets whose job is to protect this man they hate. Five thousand troops stand at Pilate's command. You can search the land of Judea and you will find no ruler more powerful. He wielded absolute power.

Pilate had likely taken the conventional route through the ranks of Roman civil service. He had probably distinguished himself as a military commander until Caesar Tiberius rewarded him with an appointment as Governor of Judea. He was the hand-picked choice of imperial Rome's emperor. Yet, despite this, you will find nothing about him in the secular history books, except perhaps a mention in an inconsequential footnote. We know Pilate lived primarily because the Bible, a book whose Lord he denied, raises Pilate to two millennia among the internationally infamous. It tells about his moment and a decision that lasts for all time. It affects you and me and everyone we love. It is ironic that Pilate's biographers were people he hated: people called Matthew, Mark, Luke, John, and Paul. We know nothing of Pilate's birth, origin, or early years. We have no way of saying for sure who, if anyone, might have been pushing his career from behind the scenes. The only things we know about him are what the Bible's human authors tell us. Beside that, his names give us what additional information we might speculate about the man. Pontius was among the most noble of Roman names. It means one destined to gallant, noble leadership. It was not a common name. The lower classes in Rome dared not give it to their children, and so we assume Pilate came from a higher level in that society. He started out well.

Pontius finds its root in the same place as the word pontificate, meaning "to speak pompously as one with authority." Perhaps government leadership and military service ran in Pilate's family. Certainly that name was one well suited for a man in Pilate's position. From the first day he arrived in Judea, Pilate spoke with the authority of Caesar. In truth, however, behind his façade he was more akin to that French cheese that almost bears his name, "Pont l-'Eveque." It's a cheese that looks good on the outside and feels hard at first touch. At its center, however, its substance is soft, runny, and sometimes even a bit gooey. That's the kind of personality we see behind the Bible references to Pilate. He looked good in his high-class Roman garb, but behind it all was a man who lacked a moral spine.

Why, then, of all the people Jesus Christ ever encountered, is Pontius Pilate's name the only one singled out for mention in the *Life Lines* of the Apostles' Creed? If it were a hall-of-shame personality from Christ's earthly life the Creed authors wanted to name, why not choose Judas Iscariot who betrayed him with a kiss, Caiaphas the crooked high priest, or another under whom Jesus suffered? Conversely, why not give mention to the name of one of those who walked side-by-side with the Master through the years of his ministry and died for his cause? Andrew would have been a good one, for example. You may remember that he was the first disciple to bring another to Jesus. Andrew was the rock before the rock called

Peter. *"We have found the Messias" (John 1:41)*, Andrew called out to Peter and beckoned his brother to come and follow the Master. Isn't that a wonderful demonstration of what Christian faith involves at its core? Why not another among the faithful? Or, even a latter-day convert with a great conversion story such as Paul? Why do we have to recite Pontius Pilate's name every time we say the Creed? We'll find out why later in this chapter. First, however, there are other important truths for us to learn.

THE CHOICE THAT CHANGED THE WORLD

In the last chapter, we noted the correctness of Larry King's assessment that if Christ were virgin born it would change everything about the world. Something else also changed the world. It was Pontius Pilate's choice of who to free between a renowned troublemaker and the Son of God. Pilate, given the opportunity to worship the true God, cast his lot somewhere among the Baals. From early in his encounter with Jesus, the Roman governor knew that Jesus Christ had done nothing wrong. Three times he declared, *"I find no fault in him...no fault at all" (cf. John 18:38; John 19:4,6)*. Pilate became an ineffective defender of the Son of God. Moreover, he finally declared Jesus *"King" (see John 19:15)*. Despite that, when push came to shove, Pilate lacked the courage to do the right thing. He had the final authority over the death penalty in Judea. No cross was erected and nobody died on one without Pontius Pilate signing off on it. He could have halted Christ's crucifixion with a word.

THE PILATES OF THE MORNING PAPER

One need look no further than the morning newspapers on almost any day to find stories that remind us of Pilate. These words are being written early in an election year and moral standards are already up for grabs with some of the candidates. Meetings between first one interest group and then another cause candidates to say things that, to most straight thinking citizens, clearly are contradictory. Statements are being made one day and retracted the next with shallow-sounding apologies by leading names among the runners. Lifestyles the Bible clearly denounces are bartered into acceptability for public endorsements. High moral standards are emphasized in one place and played down in another where polls indicate they are not welcome. In a kind of salvation-by-survey environment, one cannot help but remember bold Elijah and the Baals. Where is courage in such an environment, one well may ask? We desperately need a prophet with the spiritual ear of America to raise the clarion call *"If the LORD be God, follow him: but if Baal, then follow him" (1 Kings 18:21)*.

Ask the Pilates of our generation why they decide the way they do and they always have a high-sounding ready response: "We have to learn to live together and respect each other's differences." That is the stock-in-phrase comeback when hard spiritual questions are posed. Ah, blessed tolerance! "Live and let live!" G.K. Chesterton once observed that tolerance is the word for those who do not believe anything anymore.

Jesus Christ was more tolerant than anyone who has ever lived, but he recognized that tolerance that has no limits is a very dangerous beast. The Master of grace was forced to die on one of Pilate's rough crosses because he could not be tolerated.

THE TOLERANCE OF INTOLERANCE

America is the most religiously tolerant nation in world history. A plethora of denominations and sects disagree with one another, sometimes strongly. Yet, we all somehow live amazingly well together. One does not hear about religious intolerance in the United States the way we hear of it in other parts of the world, for example in the Middle East. Yet, it exists here in a subtle disguise. Tolerance is a quality many liberal politicians and churchmen believe is uniquely theirs. At the same time, however, these very people are the ones who would silence Christ's voice in the name of tolerance. It seems easy to be blind to the fact that our tolerance can channel us straight into intolerance. Christ's voice is quieted in America's public schools in the name of tolerance. In our zeal not to offend, we have thrown out Christ and forced paganism on our schoolchildren. In the name of this strange tolerance that leads to intolerance, using the name of the Sovereign Lord of the universe is no longer acceptable in civic organizations and city council meetings, where opening prayers offered in his name were not long ago the normal way that meetings began. In the name of tolerance, Christ is not tolerated! We would never put him on a cross. We are much too polite for that. Yet, we kill him just the same because of our intolerance.

CHRIST AND CAESAR!

"If you let this man go you are not Caesar's friend." The religious leaders mixed politics and religion together for a moment, a thing they normally despised. Their weird cocktail of religion and politics was calculated as a veiled threat to force Pilate to order the end they desired for Jesus.

"Not Caesar's friend!" I have no doubt that Pilate gulped as those words took root in his consciousness. The thought of this accusation making its way somehow to Rome petrified his political sensibilities. In

my imagination, I can hear him thinking, "They're talking about my job!" Judea's governorship was not the best appointment Rome had to offer but it was not the worst either. For Pilate, it signified a career step in the right direction for one with political ambitions. It certainly was better than a job in some lesser territorial backwater. I suspect those words from the religious leaders before him put Pilate under a tighter kind of pressure than he had experienced in a while. At the moment he heard them, he consciously or unconsciously abdicated his position. In that moment, the mob effectively became Judea's collective Governor. Under that implied threat, Pilate made a call that changed the course of human history. *"When Pilate therefore heard that saying, he brought Jesus forth, and sat down in the judgment seat in a place that is called the Pavement, but in the Hebrew, Gabbatha...and he saith unto the Jews, 'Behold your King!'"* (John 19:13,14).

UP THE ORGANIZATION AND DOWN WITH JESUS

How many times have people whose lips profess Jesus as Lord backed away from him when it looked as though their jobs or incomes or futures might be threatened over holding fast to a principle? How many standards once embraced firmly have been sacrificed for a promotion at work? How many times has a blind eye or a deaf ear been turned to accommodate something that was clearly immoral or illegal or just plain wrong? Ah, the choices we make when the going gets tough!

"Immorality is the cumulative product of small indulgences and miniscule compromises."[15] What we often don't realize until it is too late is that when we make minor adjustments to our moral standards, we lay the track for a major moral fall farther down the road. Most of the people in deep sin whom I've counseled did not "pass go and go directly to jail," to borrow the phrase from a well-known board game. Instead, they took a tiny, seemingly inconsequential, step down a slippery slope and before long they ended up in a moral freefall that often cost them things they treasured dearly. They have learned the hard way that sin is never cheap. It never settles for a low-priced substitute. Sooner or later it demands a steep price. Choices made today have consequences for tomorrow, whether Pilate makes them or we do.

An absent-minded and somewhat sadistic college professor walked into his freshman biology class holding a brown bag in his hand. His students noticed that on this day there was a twinkle in his eye as he began to tease the squeamish undergraduates, saying, "Today, I will initiate you into the International Society of Dissectors. I have here a large frog, freshly caught from a pond near my home. I want you to meet him, greet him, touch him, and observe his energy and enjoyment of life. Then, when he least expects it, we shall dissect him with great pleasure and observe parts of him that shall make you glad to pass up your evening meal." He opened the bag cautiously and reached inside for its contents. To his complete horror, he pulled out a bologna sandwich and exclaimed, "But I already ate my lunch!"

In a sense, the professor's experience was a mirror reflection of what happened to Adam and Eve. They, too, found out they had eaten the wrong thing. The forbidden fruit tasted good for the moment but, after they swallowed Satan's line, they had to live with truth and its eternal consequences. The same is true for us. What tastes good in the mouth can be mighty unsettling to digest for the long term.

REPENTING OF RIGHT DOING

Of all creation, only people have the opportunity to say yes or no to God's plan for their lives. Ultimately we all face choices and ultimately we all stand among either the sheep or the goats. Pilate made his choice and suffered the consequences. No matter how well his life may have started out, he has been the subject of two thousand years of disgrace.

We had best get used to the idea that having choices in life means that our moral standards will be challenged. People who can reject temptation are a threat to those who cannot. The strategy of the cannots will be to attempt to sideline the cans by calling us intolerant and a host of other names none of us wants to be called and to threaten our existence at some level. Standards, ideals, morals, and principles that do not fit the scheme of the culture at large will be challenged. Why should it be any different? We follow one whose public standards conveyed a message his society, including its religious leaders, could not stand. That is why Pilate's name became known in the first place. Yogi Berra is credited with saying, "If you don't know where you are going, you may end up someplace else." [16] He is right! The choices we make indicate the direction our soul is taking. If we choose to follow what M. Scott Peck called "The Road Less Traveled," we should expect to be challenged, attacked, and slandered by those who follow the broad road to the peril of their eternal souls. When your challenge comes be ready to stand firm and refuse to repent of right doing. *"Unto you it is given in the behalf of Christ, not only to believe on him, but also to suffer for his sake" (Philippians 1:29).* Paul says that to suffer for choosing to do the right thing is a blessing, a gift from God.

KNOWING WHO YOU ARE

One of my favorite stories is credited to St. Augustine, who was a moral reprobate before he committed his life to Christ. It is said of him that after his conversion he was spotted in the marketplace by one of his former paramours. Delighted to see him, her mind raced with immoral possibilities and she moved with haste in Augustine's direction. Augustine, observing her approach and, from her posture, quickly sizing up what was on her mind, turned and walked away. It did not hinder her for a moment. She walked after him calling, "Augustine! Augustine!" He walked a bit faster. Breaking into a virtual trot, she outpaced him and, after she had moved in front of him, suggestively whispered, "Augustine, it is I." In response, Augustine said quietly but firmly, "I know, but it is no longer I!" He had made up his mind for Christ. He was a new man and he dared not give the old man space. Augustine knew whose he was and he would not be moved. Can you imagine how far different Augustine's life and its mark might have been had he even just that once compromised his convictions? How far different would history have been if Pontius Pilate had taken the stance Augustine took!

THE STRANGEST PHRASE

"I believe...Jesus Christ, His only Son, our Lord...Suffered under Pontius Pilate." This is surely, at least on the surface, the strangest phrase in this Creed that omits so much of Christ and his life on Earth. There is, for example, not a word about our Lord's teachings. There is no reference to the Holy Spirit descending like a dove and the Father's glorious affirmation, *"This is my beloved Son, in whom I am well pleased" (Matthew 3:17).* Nothing is said about Christ's miracles or parables that gave mudpacks healing quality and mustard seeds mountain-sized stature. There is not even a line about the apostles for whom the Creed is named. Why?

PURPOSEFUL PAIN

There are two reasons, I believe. The first is that this *Life Line* introduces us to the reality that Jesus Christ was born for suffering. There was a purpose behind Pilate's rejection. In Isaiah's words, *"It pleased the LORD to bruise him" (Isaiah 53:10).*

From the beginning, Christ's life was marked for hurt. *"There was no room for them in the inn" (Luke 2:7).* Under Pilate's predecessor, Christ made his home among the homeless the very night he entered this world. It was the beginning of a life track that would see him unidentified by his own people. Misunderstood! Maligned! Called Mary's illegitimate child! Rejected! Alienated! Betrayed! Beaten! Agonized! Heartbroken! Deprived! Kangaroo courted! Finally, abandoned by his Father! Every kind of evil that any person has ever suffered was laid on Jesus Christ and all under Pontius Pilate. Pilate had a chance to alter the course of the stream of injustice that ran through Christ's life and he blew it. "He suffered under

Pontius Pilate!" He suffered that we might be spared the suffering our sin deserves. None of us knows, or ever will know, physical or emotional suffering with which Jesus Christ cannot identify firsthand. When tough times come your way, you can know that the Son of God who loves you has been through it all. Moreover, you will learn that through his suffering he paved the way for our final victory.

THE THREE FACES OF PILATE

There is a second reason why the Creed's authors included a *Life Line* about Pontius Pilate and Christ's suffering. When I allow my imagination to look into the face of Pontius Pilate, I see not one but three faces.

The first face is that of a man of high position, one who is powerful and enviable. His purple bordered toga and snap-finger power make him look like a winner by all the standards that societies like ours use to judge a man's success. There are times when I want to be that man. If I allowed my mind to wander, there are moments when I could become consumed by a quest for position, power, possessions and what I can imagine those things can do for the people I love most. Yet, years of ministry among people who possess these things have taught me that power and possessions are no guarantee of inner peace. One wise young woman of significant wealth and influence said, "I have just enough money and power to get me into more trouble than the average person ever dreams of in a bad nightmare!"

The second face I see is that of a shortsighted man who sells his soul for another day in a Roman high place. He is a man I hate with a vengeance for what he did to my Jesus. There are times when I can imagine that I might lose control of my temper if the two of us should ever meet. If I sat on Pilate's jury, I would find no room for mercy.

About the time I hate Pilate most, a third face comes into my line of consciousness. It is the most fascinating face of all. "Was there ever another person like Pontius Pilate, the Roman governor of Judea?" I asked earlier in this chapter. The answer is "There was and there is." This is the real reason why Pilate rates this infamous line. He rates mention over Judas, Caiaphas, and all the other despicable personalities with whom Christ came into contact because Pontius Pilate stands in the place of the whole Gentile world. Christ himself said, *"All things that are written by the prophets concerning the Son of man shall be accomplished. For he shall be delivered unto the Gentiles, and shall be mocked, and spitefully entreated, and spitted on: And they shall scourge him, and put him to death" (Luke 18:31-33).* My problem with the third face is that it is the face of a man like me, a non-Jew of European heritage, a heathen, a sinner, whom the psalmist in his prophecy called a dog (see Psalm 22:16).

Do not hear Pontius Pilate's name as we normally pronounce it when we say the Creed. Hear it instead as he most likely said it, with an emphasis on the final vowel. Pil-aht-ay! Jesus Christ, God's sinless Son, suffered not under a Jewish religious leader but under a man whose ethnicity was akin to mine and perhaps yours. Like me, Pontius Pilate could look very good and act very bad. Like me, he had many opportunities to do good but ended up doing things he will always hate. When I see this face, I cry out with that publican of whom Jesus spoke, *"God be merciful to me a sinner!" (Luke 18:13)*. In that instant, I know I need Isaiah's suffering servant to redeem me by his precious blood shed on Pilate's wicked cross.

Truth is, we all have some of Pilate in us. Pilate was not alone in killing Christ. I was there, too. Weren't you? If you are honest, you will admit that you were. The good news is that Pilate not only executed Jesus, he also executed God's grace-filled plan for our redemption. Let us then, as a response of deep gratitude, resolve from this day forward that, God helping us, we shall stand away from the crowd and choose the narrow way of God's beloved Son, our Savior.

In the next chapter, we shall consider the full force of what it meant for Christ to die on our behalf. Read on, and let your heart absorb an undeniable truth that will raise it to new heights of gratitude.

CHAPTER TEN

What Is the Greatest Love Story in History?

"How Deep is Your Love?"
That title to a song that topped the record charts a few years back echoes a question that has been on the minds of songwriters for generations. How far will true love go? The final measure of love's depth is not how often it is told but the extent to which it will go. Love is more than a concept. It is more than words. "God so loved the world, that he gave" (John 3:16). At its heart, love is a verb, an action word. This chapter brings us face-to-face with the final depth to which love will go. Read on and your heart will soar with gratitude.

The student had just returned from her Easter recess when she approached a beloved Bible professor with her question: "Our preacher said that on the first Good Friday, Jesus really just swooned on the cross and the disciples revived him and nursed him back to health. What do you think?" The wise old professor, tongue in check, replied, "Next time you go home give your preacher thirty-nine lashes with a cat-o'-nine-tails. After that, make him lie down on a cross and nail him to it. When he is securely fastened, raise the cross with him on it and drop the bottom of its main beam into a deep hole. Leave him hanging out there in the afternoon sun for several hours. Along the way, run a spear through his heart, and when he looks dead, embalm him and place him in a musty, damp tomb for a couple of days and see what happens!"

At the core of the Apostles' Creed lies one *Life Line* that pictures death and that locks us head on with the heart of the gospel: "I believe...Jesus Christ was Crucified, Dead, and Was Buried."

THE PREACHING OF THE CROSS

Winston Churchill is one of my life heroes. I can listen for hours to the scratchy recordings of his oratory and come away inspired every time. In my library, I have all his books and perhaps every book ever written about him. Cast symbols of his round, pugnacious face complete with cigar adorn my bookshelves both at home and in my study at the church. I grew up hearing the tales of "Mr. Churchill" and the way he inspired the people of the United Kingdom to victory when all the odds seemed against them winning World War II. Stories about Sir Winston always hold my attention. One of my favorites comes from a conversation that took place soon after he lost the first general election following that war where he played a key role in bringing about victory over Hitler's tyranny. In that setting, a contemporary of Churchill's came to encourage the defeated Prime Minister that his usefulness had not ended. "You could," said Churchill's friend, "redirect your considerable oratorical skills towards preaching." As the story was first told to me, Churchill's immediate response was, "Any man who thinks he has the ability to bring the same message to the same audience week after week and hold their attention is a fool. I may have lost the election but I am not a fool!" It was, perhaps, the most thoughtless answer Sir Winston Churchill ever gave for it portrayed his apparent inability to distinguish between preaching and oratory. In failing to recognize the difference, Sir Winston is perhaps not alone. Others seem to have missed the distinction, too.

The difference is really very simple. It is that good oratory can be delivered about almost any subject. Good preaching, on the other hand, always leads to the cross and the crucifixion of Jesus. An orator's principle role is to deliver his message in such a way that the listeners will understand and believe what he says, while a preacher must add to that the necessity of communicating Christ's cross. Without the cross, oratory, no matter how well done, is not a sermon. Charles Haddon Spurgeon, one of history's finest preachers in the English-speaking world, told his students, "When you mount the pulpit, read your text then jump over the hedges and span every ditch until you bring your congregation face-to-face with Christ's cross." He also told them, "Let it be your ambition so to declare God's word that the people will say not, 'What an excellent preacher, but, 'How glorious his Christ!'"

It was a large banquet and the elderly minister was surprised to find himself invited to offer an invocation. He was even more surprised when he was seated at the head table next to a well-known actor, famous for his oratory. The actor and the pastor introduced themselves to one another and immediately became friends. The master of ceremonies, noticing the celebrity's presence, invited him to come to the podium. After a few flattering remarks, the toastmaster, caught up in his moment with a celebrity, gushingly asked the actor if he would honor the group by giving a brief invocation. The distinguished guest hesitated and said he did not feel qualified to do it. The old minister, trying to save his new friend from this embarrassing moment, handed the orator his Bible, which he had opened at Psalm 23. In an undertone he whispered, "Here, read the Twenty-third Psalm." The man knew the words and with passion born of years of study, recited those six thrilling verses with such a resonant voice and pathos that at the close a subdued expression of approval rang through the audience. Unexpectedly, the actor then invited the elderly pastor to stand and read them. When the old man of God finished, many eyes were filled with tears, for he spoke not with learned pathos and oratorical skill but with warmth, tenderness, and deep personal understanding. The actor listened intently and, with tears in his eyes, said afterward, "He did it far better than I, not so much because he is more familiar with the psalm, but because he knows the Shepherd." Oratory draws attention to the speaker. Preaching directs its focus toward the Shepherd and his love demonstrated on the cross.

"The preaching of the cross is to them that perish foolishness; but unto us which are saved it is the power of God" (1 Corinthians 1:18). The crucifixion of our leader makes Christians different from the devotees of every other great religious leader in world history. Nobody but Jesus died in the place of his disciples. A preacher's first responsibility before Almighty God is to deliver the message of Christ's cross in a different envelope every time he or she preaches.

THE DISFAVORED CROSS

Soon after I arrived in Pittsburgh, an advertising man suggested that I was making too much mention of the cross in my sermons. His argument, he said, was based on recent research in his industry. "The cross is an unpopular topic with people today," he told me. I acknowledged his good intentions, thanked him for his advice, and reminded him that the devil in Adolf Hitler found the cross unattractive, too. Hitler's Third Reich expressly declared that one of its principle goals was to remove every church cross in Europe and replace it with the swastika, which, interestingly enough, was once a pagan cross. Why would they do that, except that they could not stand the cross?

That should not surprise us. The cross has always been an offense and a stumbling block. It was the ugliest form of death Rome's cruelest leaders could imagine. For them it had a double-barreled impact. It represented both punishment and prevention. Not only was it an instrument of death and disgrace, it was also an instrument of warning. To all who passed by, it said, "Behave or end up here!"

On the other hand, there is a certain irony about the current unpopularity about the cross. A Jewish jeweler friend of mine showed me an article he had clipped from a leading women's magazine not long ago. It said that a cross is the most desirable item of jewelry in a woman's wardrobe today and suggested that the well-dressed woman will likely possess several different crosses, each to be worn according to the occasion or the outfit. It even referred to the cross as a religious "plus-sign."

I thought about that again last week when I visited one of our local Christian bookstores and observed a clerk remove some Bibles from a prominent display shelf in order to make room for something called "Promise Pops." Each of these pops is imprinted with an upbeat verse of Scripture that can be sucked away. Now, I like pops but only a real sucker would ever think that a lollipop could ever take the place of God's word. There were other cheap, gaudy trinkets and cute looking play pieces there, too. Looking a little closer, I spotted some crosses on display in a jewelry case. They looked nice until I saw these words on a sign beside them, "Genuine Gold Plate."

What a contradiction in terms the words "Genuine gold plate" compose. They say, in effect, "This is an authentic imitation of the real thing." The crosses looked shiny on the outside but underneath they were something else. Tragically, that also seems to be a good summation of many who profess the name of Christ. A leader in the National Prayer Breakfast movement described a certain well-known politician as "a Christian who puts his political party ahead of everything else." That sounds like a gold-plate theology to me. No matter how loudly that man professes Jesus Christ, the fact is that ultimately the party owns his soul. Unless he changes his priorities, he will end up in the company of Pontius Pilate, who, as we saw in the last chapter, allowed his job to take precedence over the life of Jesus.

If you are seeking faith that looks good only on the surface, you will not find it in following Jesus Christ. Being one of his disciples requires more than such a superficial commitment. Discipleship, as expressed in the New Testament, can be very demanding. Yet, there are still preachers who market such a trinket message to unsuspecting ears. Theirs is a gospel of feel-good-ism, incompatible with the message Jesus preached. Its key focus is "me" and "mine," "you" and "yours." It calls for no real commitment except that which serves the preacher. It needs to remember the words of St. Francis de Sales, who declared, "The test of a great preacher is not that the congregation goes away saying, 'What a lovely sermon,' but, 'I will do something!'"

Near the end of World War II, Dietrich Bonhoeffer wrote a message from a Nazi prison camp where he was being held, and finally hanged, for preaching the message of the cross in the face of Nazi tyranny. He entitled his message, "Costly Grace." In it, he compares the grace of the Bible with this cheap grace proffered by some preachers. He writes, "Cheap grace is the deadly enemy of the church…Cheap grace means grace sold on the market like cheap-jack's wares. The sacraments, the forgiveness of sin, and the consolations of religion are thrown away at cut prices."[17]

Be assured that Christ's crucifixion on the cross was not any cut-rate sacrifice, nor was it any gilded-edged, near-death experience for him. He really died. He was as dead as death can make a man. How dead was he? The next chapter will tell us "He descended into hell." He did not swoon. He did not pretend. He was not nursed back to health by the disciples and the women who were closest to him. He died for you on a real Roman cross.

THE FATHER AND THE CROSS

It was May 1953, and the world listened in awe as New Zealander Edmund Hillary and his Nepalese guide, Tensing Norkay, made it all the way to the summit of Mount Everest, 29,023 feet above sea level. Man had conquered the highest peak on Earth. For God the Father, Earth's highest peak was not Mount Everest but Mount Calvary. Calvary is nowhere near 29,023 feet high. It is not even as high as some of the beautiful hills around the city of Pittsburgh. What makes Calvary higher than Everest for God is that it was on Calvary that God planted a cross to demonstrate how high his love for us would go to bring about our redemption. Perhaps you are already protesting that the cross on which Jesus died was a Roman instrument. If so, you are only right to a limited extent. That rude instrument of final punishment set up at the command of Rome was, in fact, first erected in the mind of God the Father long before there was a Rome. John sees this in the Revelation, when he calls Jesus *"the Lamb slain from the foundation of the world" (Revelation 13:8).*

Before the creation, God, who is omniscient, knew that even his whole creation would not satisfy humanity's compulsive desire to break out of the boundaries, so he made provision for our redemption. *"He hath chosen us in him before the foundation of the world, that we should be holy and without blame before him in love: Having predestinated us unto the adoption of children by Jesus Christ to himself, according to the good pleasure of his will, To the praise of the glory of his grace, wherein he hath made us accepted in the beloved. In whom we have redemption through his blood, the forgiveness of sins, according to the riches of his grace" (Ephesians 1:3-7).* It was on God's mind that something as drastic as a crucifixion must come about to save us in our sins. For that reason, we can say that the cross was God the Father's idea before Rome was born. It was the only way that he could remain just and become the justifier of the unjust.

Being a grandfather is the most expensive hobby I have ever had! I should hasten to add that it is also the most rewarding. What is more, one does not have to wait for the birth of one's grandchildren to become an enthusiast. Before Hannah or Cameron, our little granddaughters were born, I remember making plans and consulting with Barbara about what we could do for them. Perhaps you can identify with that because of children or grandchildren in your life. As we anxiously count down the days to the child's arrival, we dream about what he or she might become and we change the focus of our lives. Suddenly, stores that specialize in baby clothes, which only a month or two before were hardly noticed, become vital pit stops on almost every visit to the mall. All our plans for our children are good. Nobody ever imagines bringing a child into the world for anything less than that. We want to give our children the best that we can in every area of life. God the Father was different. As he contemplated the birth of his son in Bethlehem, God was not thinking in the normal realms. He knew that his son would be unwelcome from the beginning. There would be no room for him neither in the inn nor among his own people. *"He came unto his own, and his own received him not" (John 1:12).* He would be *"despised and rejected of men; a man of sorrows, and acquainted with grief" (Isaiah 53:3).* And he would be crucified between two thieves. All of this began in the mind of the Father. That is a love such as we have never given and have never received from any other source. The cross was built by Rome but the Father designed it.

GOD'S KISS

A woman invited her little nephew who did not attend church to join her in worship one Sunday. Afterward, the family asked him how he liked it and what impressed him the most. Immediately he replied, "It was God's kiss." "What?" his intrigued company asked him. "God's kiss," he repeated, then added, "I saw it on one of the windows. God was carrying a big kiss on his shoulders." Now they were beginning to catch on, especially as he added, "You know, when I send a card to Grandma or one of you, I always add a kiss under my name. God was carrying a kiss like that, except it was a lot bigger." He was right. That cross carried by the Son was the Father's kiss to all of us. His Son was "crucified, dead and buried."

THE PAIN OF THE CROSS

During a visit to St. Louis, Missouri, Pope John Paul II called the death penalty a sin. His rationale was based on reports that the death penalty administered in the United States today is a cruel form of punishment. As a gesture of respect, Missouri's governor commuted the death sentence of a murderer who was scheduled to die the same week the Pope was in town.

Is the death penalty a sin? Or, does Scripture provide the governing authorities a warrant to apply the death penalty? Good theologians stand on both sides of that argument and answering it here goes far beyond the realms of this book. Suffice it to say today's death penalty, as administered in the United States, brings relatively little physical pain, although no one would argue that it is emotionally painful for those who receive it and those who love them.

The pain of crucifixion in first century Jerusalem was different. Emotional? Rome had no more shame-filled punishment. There was a stigma attached to it that lasted far longer for family members than the physical pain endured by the one who was hanged. The physical pain was not polite either. The person to be crucified, having received the prescribed scourging with a Roman cat-o'-nine-tails, was forced to lie flat, his slashed flesh forced against two rough-hewn crossbeams that were placed flat on the ground. Jagged nails made from hardwood were driven through the wrists and near the ankles. The ankles were placed one on top of the other to make them fit the vertical beam of the cross and to prevent the person on the cross from leaning weight first on one side then the other as a means of seeking temporary relief. Once the subject was firmly pinned to the cross beams, the cross was raised vertically and jarred into a hole that had been dug deep into the ground. This tore the flesh and brought further excruciating pain to an already scourged body. This unnatural position multiplied the agony of any movements the person on the cross might try to make to gain relief. The crucified one's lacerated veins and crushed tendons throbbed with incessant pain. It is no wonder that during this process many victims fainted from the pain alone, and perhaps this is what gives proponents of the "swoon theory" of Christ's crucifixion their notion that Christ did not really die.[18]

The wounds of the subjects on the cross, inflamed by exposure to filth, became gangrenous. The arteries of the head swelled with surcharged blood and throbbed with agony. The blazing afternoon sun provoked a burning, raging thirst. After a while, the legs of the person on the cross were usually broken by a sharp blow from a log about the thickness of a baseball bat. This prevented the crucified one from trying to ease the intense pain by raising his body using what little strength might remain in his knee joints. Christ's legs were not broken because he was already dead. This was in fulfillment of the prophesy, *"He keepeth all his bones: not one of them is broken" (Psalm 34:20).*

Cross patrol was a roughneck assignment for a soldier in the Roman army. There was no honor to it. It may even have been the most undesirable duty of all. Usually it was a punishment for some offense. The mission was so ghastly that soldiers were given strong drink to numb their senses. Despite that, or perhaps because of it, Roman legionnaires often were sick to their stomachs as they carried out their cruel task. It was not unusual for them to be unable to keep food down for days afterward as they reflected on what they had done. The Son of God hung in that kind of company as he thought of us and died.

THE POMP OF THE CROSS

"God forbid that I should glory, save in the cross of our Lord Jesus Christ, by whom the world is crucified unto me, and I unto the world" (Galatians 6:14).

The crucifixion of Jesus has a glory of its own in that it demonstrates how deep the Father's love is for us. As I write these words, our first-born, Gary, is about the age Jesus was when he died. I confess that I could never give up Gary for anything or anyone in the world. This year, as never before, I have a new understanding of John 3:16: *"God so loved the world, that he gave his only begotten Son, that whosoever believeth in him should not perish, but have everlasting life."*

Another glory of the cross is that it covers over all our sin and all our sins. Sin (singular) is what we are. Sins (plural) are what we do because of what we are. We are helplessly entangled in sin and so we commit sins. The cross proclaims across the centuries that God *"loved us, and sent his Son to be the propitiation for our sins" (1 John 4:10).* Are you living free of shame? Christ's death on the cross made shame-free living possible for all of us.

The lasting glory of the cross is that when this life is over we shall not die because Jesus, our Savior, *"brought life and immortality to light through the gospel" (2 Timothy 1:10).*

"He was crucified, dead, and was buried." Yet, Christ did not die alone that day on Calvary; death died, too. *"O death, where is thy sting? O grave, where is thy victory?...Thanks be to God, which giveth us the victory through our Lord Jesus Christ" (1 Corinthians 15:55,57).*

I believe this because the Bible teaches it. Christ died and Christ went to hell. In the next chapter, we will look at one of the great controversial *Life Lines* of the Apostles' Creed. Read on and learn the depths that Christ has plumbed on our behalf.

CHAPTER ELEVEN

Is There a Hell?

Where did Jesus go after he died? Is hell a real place? Think about it: Week in and week out, for the best part of twenty centuries, generations of Christians have recited the Apostles' Creed. Multiplied millions of times, Christians have professed their belief that Jesus "descended into hell." Yet, a few years ago a number of mainline denominations published a new hymnbook that omitted this line from the Creed. They did so, they said, because many leading professors of theology called this Life Line unbelievable. Is it a lie to say Jesus descended into hell? Or, is it one of the great mysterious truths of the faith? What difference does it make in your life today whether or not it is true? Read on and discover for yourself.

WHERE GRIM AND GLORY MEET

It is a grim and glorious *Life Line* that gets our attention in this chapter. "I believe...Jesus Christ, his only Son, our Lord...descended into hell." No line in the Creed, or perhaps in Christian theology, has been more controversial. We would prefer to confess that Jesus suffered under Pontius Pilate, was crucified, died, was buried, and rose gloriously into paradise. But that is not an option.

93

The whole idea of hell is decidedly out of style in our pseudo-sophisticated Elijah generation, so it should be no surprise that we have a particular mental discomfort with the idea of God's Son going there. Ours is an age in which many profess that they choose to create their own small g gods from a plethora of religious fantasies. Almost always these gods made by us make it possible for everyone upon death to enter a realm of splendor and eternal joy. The final outcome of all man-made religions sounds universally good. I dare suggest that you have never heard of a cult group that had much to say about hell. They generally speak of only positive eternal outcomes, sometimes with various levels of transcendent blessing. If only that were true!

Even in the church, we are uncomfortable with the idea of a loving God allowing anyone or (perish the thought!) consigning anyone, much less his Son, to hell. This was not always the case. The old preachers often were satirized as hate-filled merchants of "hell fire and brimstone." We have traveled, for the most part, a long way from that. Church historian Martin Marty says that the notion of hell is "culturally unavailable" in our society.[19] Heaven is far more pleasant to dream about, and we don't like to think about the existence of hell or that anyone we know belongs there. Or, if we do, we want to have a say in who should be hell's residents. Hell is okay for Adolf Hitler, Idi Amin, Saddam Hussein, and Charles Manson; it is an acceptable eternal address for Karl Marx and other mis-shapers of human destinies; but it is not acceptable for the regular folks who live around us and whom we perceive to be lesser sinners.

I grew up not far from the Bronte family homestead in Northern Ireland, and much of what the Bronte sisters wrote was required reading from the earliest days of my formal schooling. In Charlotte Bronte's *Jane Eyre,* Jane, as a young orphan, is questioned by the insensitive Reverend Brocklehurst in one of the opening scenes. In his efforts to determine Jane's eligibility to matriculate in boarding school, the ruthless reverend begins his inquisition:

"Your name, little girl?" asks Rev. Brocklehurst sternly as he begins the inquisition.

"Jane Eyre, sir."

"Well, Jane Eyre, are you a good child?"

Jane hesitates because she knows that she is not a "good child," but it will hardly do to admit that she is a naughty little girl. Her aunt intervenes: "Perhaps the less said on that subject the better, Mr. Brocklehurst."

The minister then calls the orphan to stand in front of the chair where he is seated. "Do you know where the wicked go after death?" he asks menacingly.

"They go to hell," she replies.

"And what is hell? Can you tell me that?"

"A pit full of fire."

"And should you like to fall into that pit, and to be burning there forever?"

"No, sir."

"What must you do to avoid it?"

This was a subject Jane had not covered in catechism, so she was on uncertain ground when she answered, "I must keep in good health and not die." [20]

PREACHERS AND PAGANS

If only it were so simple! A friend of mine tells of hearing a young preacher say in a sermon to his congregation, "If you will not believe in Jesus Christ, you will suffer grave eschatological consequences." An old gentleman asked, "Preacher, do you mean that if we don't follow Jesus Christ we will go to hell?" "Precisely," the preacher replied. "Well," responded the old man, "why don't you just say that?"

Hearing that reminded me of a story told to me after I spoke at a conference for Second World War veterans. A group of GIs sailing across the English Channel toward D-Day asked their troopship chaplain if he believed in hell. The chaplain exclaimed, "Of course, not! It's old-fashioned." "Then, chaplain," responded one tough sergeant, "with all due respect, you should resign your commission. For if there is no hell, we don't need you here with a Prayer Book but with a rifle. On the other hand, if there is, you are leading these men astray."

Those soldiers were better biblical theologians than their assigned spiritual leader. They could see that so long as there is no hell, whatever feels good is inconsequential behavior and the Christian gospel is irrelevant nostalgia. If hell does not exist, the cross is an unnecessary castigation and Jesus Christ is a poor misled fool for hanging on it. What is the point of his pain and suffering detailed in the previous chapter if there is, finally, nothing from which Christ needed to save us? Billy Sunday was neither reticent like the young preacher nor misguided like the chaplain. He frequently preached, "Hell is the highest reward that the devil can offer you for being a servant of his."

Interestingly enough, the dying words of some of history's great infidels speak more clearly of hell than either those of the young preacher or the chaplain. Thomas Hobbes, the English political theorist and unbeliever whom King Charles II protected from facing heresy charges, is said to have cried out as he died, "I am taking a fearful leap into the dark." French Enlightenment leader Francois-Marie Arouet Voltaire, who denounced the church, is reputed to have died saying, "I am abandoned by God and man; I shall go to hell." Sir Francis Newport, another outspoken unbeliever and opponent of the gospel, wailed, "Oh that I could lie a thousand years upon the fire that is never quenched, to purchase the favor of God and be united to him again. But, it is a fruitless wish. Oh, eternity, eternity forever and forever! Oh, the insufferable pangs of hell!" Charlie Peace was one of the most violent criminals England ever produced. As he walked toward the gallows on the day he was hanged, he heard a minister reading from the Bible. He stopped momentarily to listen. The clergyman was reading about heaven and hell. Peace interrupted the preacher saying, "Sir, if I believed what you and the church of God say, even if England were covered with broken glass from coast to coast, I would walk over it on hands and knees and think it worthwhile living just to save one soul from an eternal hell like that."[21] These and many others who denied belief in God preached better sermons as they died than some of us do as we live.

Do you believe in hell? If not, are you surprised to learn that Jesus, the one person in all history in the best position to know whether hell is real, the only one who never told a lie, was not shy when he spoke about hell? At least fifteen times in the gospels he speaks about hell as a living reality. He believed in it, spoke about it, and preached to warn his hearers against it. You can read it all through the gospels of Matthew, Mark, Luke, and John. For example, *"When the Son of man shall come in his glory, and all the holy angels with him, then shall he sit upon the throne of his glory: And before him shall be gathered all nations: and he shall separate them one from another, as a shepherd divideth his sheep from the goats: And he shall set the sheep on his right hand, but the goats on the left. Then shall the King say unto them on his right hand, 'Come, ye blessed of my Father, inherit the kingdom prepared for you from the foundation of the world: For I was an hungered, and ye gave me meat: I was thirsty, and ye gave me drink: I was a stranger, and ye took me in: Naked, and ye clothed me: I was sick, and ye visited me: I was in prison, and ye came unto me.' Then shall the righteous answer him, saying, 'Lord, when saw we thee an hungered, and fed thee? or thirsty, and gave thee drink? When saw we thee a stranger, and took thee in? or naked, and clothed thee? Or when saw we thee sick, or in prison, and came unto thee?' And the King shall answer and say unto them, 'Verily I say unto you, Inasmuch as ye have done it unto one of the least of these my brethren, ye have done it unto me.' Then shall he say also unto them on the left hand, 'Depart from me, ye cursed, into everlasting fire, prepared for the devil and his angels: For I was an hungered, and ye gave me no meat: I was thirsty, and ye gave me no drink: I was a stranger, and ye took me not in: naked, and ye clothed me not: sick, and in prison, and ye visited me not.' Then shall they also answer him, saying, 'Lord, when saw we thee an hungered, or athirst, or a stranger, or naked, or sick, or in prison, and did not minister unto thee?' Then shall he answer them, saying, 'Verily I say unto you, Inasmuch as ye did it not to one* of the least of these, ye did it not to me. And these shall go away into everlasting punishment: but the righteous into life eternal'" (Matthew 25:31-46).

What is more, the Bible speaks, both explicitly and implicitly, about Christ being in hell: "Thou wilt not leave my soul in hell; neither wilt thou suffer thine Holy One to see corruption" (Psalm 16:10; cf 1 Corinthians 15:20). "If I ascend up into heaven, thou art there: if I make my bed in hell, behold, thou art there" (Psalm 139:8). "When the sixth hour was come, there was darkness over the whole land until the ninth hour. And at the ninth hour Jesus cried with a loud voice, saying, Eloi, Eloi, lama sabachthani? which is, being interpreted, My God, my God, why hast thou forsaken me?" (Mark 15:33,34). Christ knows what hell is like from firsthand experience. He endured hell for us.

NO FRIENDS IN HELL

A legendary Irish cemetery has a tombstone that bears this epitaph:

> Pause stranger when you pass me by,
> As you are now, so once was I
> As I am now, so you will be,
> So prepare for death and follow me.

Some wise wag read those words and inscribed a wooden board with this answer, which he erected in the soil beside that grave:

> To follow you I'm not content,
> Until I find out where you went!

What is hell like? "The mind in its own place, and in itself can make a Heav'n of Hell, a Hell of Heav'n," says John Milton in *Paradise Lost*. There are many pictures in Scripture. It is a place of judgment and eternal damnation. It is not the kind of place anyone in his right mind would want to go.

The comedians have had a heyday with hell. A story tells about a well-known comedian bantering with a New York City street preacher whose sermon alluded to hell as a place of teeth gnashing. "Sir, I have no teeth," the comedian called out, seeking to gain attention for himself. "Don't worry, sir," the preacher responded without losing a breath, "for people like you, teeth will be provided!"

For Christ, and for us, the worst part of hell is that it is a place of abject loneliness, a barren location where there is no contact with anyone, not even God. "Eloi, Eloi, lama sabachthani? which is, being interpreted, My God, my God, why hast thou forsaken me?" (Mark 15:34). On the cross, Jesus entered that realm where no one could embrace and comfort him in his suffering, not even his Father.

Ask any pastor. Personal experience confirmed by the testimonies of our parishioners tells us that no human misery equals that of prolonged loneliness. Yet, even the lonely on Earth have the promise of Christ's companionship when no other person is about. However, in hell it will be different, for hell is finally an eternally God-forsaken environment. Jesus experienced hell for us.

Some time ago I presented the gospel to a fellow who came into our church asking for help. When I invited him to receive Christ and know assurance of eternal life in heaven, he was unusually forthright in his response. "I don't want to go to heaven," he retorted. "I want to go to hell and be with all my friends." I reminded him that that is not possible because part of hell's eternal punishment is abject, irresolvable loneliness. No one in hell will ever see or fellowship with another person again. There are no "friends" there. The one security of hell is "I am on my own." Thomas Merton said, "Hell is where no one has anything in common with anybody else except the fact that they all hate one another."

CHRIST'S MISSION INTO HELL

The authors of the current version of the Apostles' Creed do not demonstrate any reticence to speak of hell with clarity: "He descended into hell." While, so far as we know, this line was not included in the old Roman form of the Creed written around A.D. 341, it appears plainly in the received form, written about fifty years after that. And so, for all the centuries, this line, often disputed and hard to understand, still stands.

C.S. Lewis writes, "Only the Greatest of all can make Himself small enough to enter Hell. For the higher a thing is, the lower it can descend—a man can sympathize with a horse but a horse cannot sympathize with a rat. Only One has descended into Hell. And will He ever do so again? It was not once long ago that He did it. Time does not work that way once ye have left the Earth. All moments that have been or shall be were, or are, present in the moment of his descending. There is no spirit in prison to whom He did not preach."[22] Christ's mission into hell was eternal in the sense that when he entered hell, he entered an eternal timelessness akin to that which he left when he came to Earth thirty-three years before he died on the cross. It was not eternal in that it was the end of life for him. *"He went and preached unto the spirits in prison" (1 Peter 3:19).*

The Greek text adds light to Peter's words. The word *kerusso,* which he uses here, means "to herald, proclaim, announce, preach." In hell, Jesus proclaimed God's gospel. You will note that *kerusso* does not imply that Jesus went to hell to evangelize. Some groups and sects disliked the concept of hell so much that they invented a notion of a second chance at salvation. All kinds of unbiblical ideas are built around this false hypothesis. One prominent one is that some sort of limbo or purgatory exists where people can be salvaged from hell after they die. Nothing in Scripture gives us reason to believe in a second-chance salvation like that. To the contrary, everything the Bible says is present tense and urgent: *"Behold, now is the accepted time; behold, now is the day of salvation" (2 Corinthians 6:2). "Today if ye will hear his voice, harden not your hearts" (Hebrews 4:7).* The focus is today, not tomorrow or some later time. *"Sow to yourselves in righteousness, reap in mercy; break up your fallow ground: for it is time to seek the LORD" (Hosea 10:12).*

The call and comfort of the gospel is always that we can know today that we have heaven and not hell as our eternal home. We do not have to wait to find out. We can know it for certain now. *"These things have I written unto you that believe on the name of the Son of God; that ye may know that ye have eternal life" (1 John 5:13).*

Christ's first reason for going to hell was to conduct a preaching mission. If he did not go to evangelize, what was his message? John Calvin suggests that Christ preached the certainty of his eternal victory and hell's eternal doom. That Dr. Calvin, who urges his students so forcefully to preach only the explicit truths of the Bible, comes to this conclusion is a source of fascination for me because the Bible never expressly says this. However, I believe he is probably right on this point.

This we do know for certain, because the Bible says it: God long before demonstrated patience with those who heard his Son preach in hell. *"He went and preached unto the spirits in prison; Which sometime were disobedient, when once the longsuffering of God waited in the days of Noah (1 Peter 3:19,20).* One day, however, God's patience ran out. Scripture warns us, *"The LORD said, 'My spirit shall not always strive with man'" (Genesis 6:3).* God's tolerance has limits. That is why we must heed the urgent call of his invitation to be saved. *"Seek ye the LORD while he may be found, call ye upon him while he is near: Let the wicked forsake his way, and the unrighteous man his thoughts: and let him return unto the LORD, and he will have mercy upon him; and to our God, for he will abundantly pardon" (Isaiah 55:6,7).* If you have not already done it, while there is time come quickly to this God of pardoning grace.

The second reason Christ descended to hell was to pay the full penalty our sins demanded. The Bible calls this *"the second death"*: *"the fearful, and unbelieving, and the abominable, and murderers, and whoremongers, and sorcerers, and idolaters, and all liars, shall have their part in the lake which burneth with fire and brimstone: which is the second death" (Revelation 21:8).* It is this death we should fear rather than the physical death with which we are more familiar because of the passing of our loved ones. Christ removed the second death's sting when, from the cross, he cried, *"My God, my God, why hast thou forsaken me?"*

Because of this we live with confidence every day knowing that we shall never die. What a difference this makes when issues that threaten ordinary people come into our lives, as they often do. That is why I began this chapter saying that this is a grim and glorious *Life Line*. It was grim for Jesus but glorious for us in that it guarantees us ultimate victory. *"Blessed and holy is he that hath part in the first resurrection: on such the second death hath no power, but they shall be priests of God and of Christ, and shall reign with him a thousand years" (Revelation 20:6)*. The power of the second death was robbed when Jesus Christ "descended into hell" for me. May you know that he descended there also for you and may you live your life in the light of his glory.

SALVATION ABC'S

How can I know this and how do I become confident of eternal life in heaven? The answer is as easy as ABC. "A" is for acknowledge. I must admit my sin and call on Christ to forgive me. "B" is for belief. To believe means to accept God's word at face value. When he says, *"God so loved the world, that he gave his only begotten Son, that whosoever believeth in him should not perish, but have everlasting life" (John 3:16)*, we believe that without question and live as though it is true. "C" is for commitment. I commit myself to renounce sin, to repent of it, and follow Christ with all my heart. Having done this, I approach the future in new power. It is the power of heaven that comes into our lives when we call Christ Lord.

In the next chapter, we shall explore the *Life Line* that makes the difference: the freeing dynamic of living faith. Does what you believe set you free or hinder you? Read on and learn how you can live the resurrected life every day.

CHAPTER TWELVE

Can We Prove Jesus Christ Rose From the Dead?

Are you a lightweight or heavyweight Christian? Does your faith free you up or tie you down? Was the death of Jesus on the cross an accident or part of God's design for world history? Can God turn evil plans into something good? In this chapter we will explore these and other questions that are central to the every day working out of what we believe. This Life Line makes a difference every day.

THE ABSOLUTE DIVIDE

Traveling through Jerusalem on one occasion, I heard about a conversation between two theologians. One was a Christian seminary teacher and the other a Moslem Imam. "We believe," said the Christian, "that God gives us three revelations of himself." The Moslem replied, "We believe that also." "The first revelation of God for us is creation," said the Christian. "And also for us," added the Imam. "Secondly," the Christian continued, "we believe God reveals himself through his holy book, the Bible." Not to be dissuaded, the Moslem replied, "We have a similar belief except that we call our holy book the Koran." The Christian affirmed, "We also believe that God has shown himself to us in a man, his Son, Jesus Christ." "We, too, believe that God is revealed in a man and he is Mohammed," said the Moslem. "We believe," said the Christian, "that the best proof that Jesus Christ substantiates his identity as God's special Son is because after he died he rose again." The Moslem's eyes fell toward the ground. He paused, then whispered in a barely audible voice, "We have no information about our man Mohammed after he died."

"I believe...Jesus Christ, his only Son, our Lord...suffered under Pontius Pilate, was crucified, died, and was buried; he descended into hell. The third day he rose again from the dead." The eternal separator among the various philosophies and religious belief systems is what they make of death. That is the theme of this latest *Life Line*.

I have just returned from the intensive care unit at a local hospital. I spent several hours over the last day or so with the family of a young woman who was dying after a life of struggle with a variety of health issues. Hers was a difficult life and her final hours on Earth were not pleasant. From a human perspective, death, although sometimes merciful, is always a very undesirable thing. The young woman's mother has known for years that her daughter might precede her in death. Yet, knowing that did not stop her from saying as she looked down at her daughter's body, "I've done everything possible to keep this day from coming." And, she did. This morning I had a telephone conversation with another mother whose recently married daughter in her mid-twenties was killed in an automobile accident. More than a year later, she still tries to reconcile what happened. Her daughter's death makes no sense. Christians are not Pollyannaish about death. We are not blind to its dreadfulness, nor insensitive about the havoc it wrecks in many lives almost every time it happens. We are very much aware of its consequences. We avoid it as much as possible. We try to cover it up with polite-sounding synonyms and well-decorated funeral services.

Yet, what sets us apart from everyone else in the world is that we have something to declare about death that no one else can say.

"Jesus Christ our Lord"... was *"declared to be the Son of God with power, according to the spirit of holiness, by the resurrection from the dead" (Romans 1:4)*. Paul's Roman letter is perhaps the finest theological treatise written in any generation. Paul met the risen Christ on the Damascus Road and a new man was born. One who once was an enemy became a fearless disciple. Now he writes to Christians living near the very seat of power at whose hands Jesus died. He writes as a Roman citizen and makes three bold declarations that distinguish what Christians believe from every other religious belief system in world history. They have implications for what we think about death and all of life.

First, says Paul, Christ's resurrection proves he is God. He was not the first one to rise from the dead. Not long before, Lazarus was raised. However, Christ's resurrection was different from Lazarus. Lazarus arose to bear again life's burdens, share its heartaches, and endure its weariness. After that, Lazarus died physically once again and was buried a second time. Christ, on the other hand, rose out of death to ascend to the Father. *"Christ being raised from the dead dieth no more; death hath no more dominion over him" (Romans 6:9).*

Second, Christ's resurrection puts new light on his death. *"If Christ be not raised, your faith is vain; ye are yet in your sins" (1 Corinthians 15:17).* Had Jesus remained dead, or had he even been raised from death like Lazarus and died again, his disciples would have quickly scattered to their own ways. They would have returned to the boats and nets of their former lives and, perhaps along with that, the scorn of their former friends. Instead, empowered by the Holy Spirit on Pentecost, they found in the resurrection new glue that bonded them together. Together, they moved the church ahead in the strength of the resurrected Lord. Without that bond, our sense of forgiveness, deliverance, hope, and new purpose for living would be groundless. The church would not exist. The Apostles' Creed would never have been written. The resurrection of Jesus makes our faith alive.

Third, Christ's resurrection points us toward the future. It directs us toward his Second Coming and judgment. *"He hath appointed a day, in the which he will judge the world in righteousness by that man whom he hath ordained; whereof he hath given assurance unto all men, in that he hath raised him from the dead" (Acts 17:31).*

How far different are the offerings of other religious systems when death is the subject under discussion. All must in some form or fashion echo the words of the Imam, "We have no information about our man after he died." Equally so is the plight of those who have no faith. If you are familiar with the teachings of Carl Sagan, who died near the end of the last century, you are aware that he was an earnest seeker after truth, or, as he preferred to call it, "proof." Carl Sagan was a disciple of science, not of faith. When physicians diagnosed his terminal illness, Carl Sagan immediately informed his friends and advised them that he did not want prayers for healing, he wanted proof. In an exchange with a minister he asked, "You're so smart, why do you believe in God?" Remembering that this was a man who believed in black holes in space that have never been observed, the minister returned his verbal volley, "Carl, you're so smart, why don't you believe in God?" After Carl Sagan died, his wife issued a public statement that said in part, "There was no deathbed conversion, no appeals to God, no hope of an afterlife, no pretending that he and I, who had been inseparable for 20 years, were not saying goodbye to each other forever." Someone asked her, "Didn't he want to believe?" She said, "Carl never wanted to believe, he wanted proof."[23]

Is there any proof that Jesus rose again from the dead? How much proof do you need? Consider these words from a former skeptic and enemy of the cross: *"Christ died for our sins according to the scriptures; And that he was buried, and that he rose again the third day according to the scriptures: And that he was seen of Cephas, then of the twelve: After that, he was seen of above five hundred brethren at once; of whom the greater part remain unto this present, but some are fallen asleep. After that, he was seen of James; then of all the apostles. And last of all he was seen of me also, as of one born out of due time"* (1 Corinthians 15:3-8).

In a moment of frustration, Michelangelo once challenged his fellow artists. "Why is it," he asked them, "that you fill gallery after gallery with portraits of Christ in abject weakness on the cross? Why do you picture him hanging as a dead man as though that were the last word we have about him? Do you not know that the cross was not the last word?" He was right! While it is true that its impact will bear fruit for all eternity, that scene of defeat and disaster that is fixed permanently in so many paintings and so many churches lasted, in fact, only a few hours. The Lord we worship in our churches is alive. He rules and reigns in triumph. He is coming again. His death was the pivotal moment in redemptive history, but we must not emphasize it to the exclusion of this: "The third day he rose again from the dead."

What does it mean for us? Recently in a graveyard in Lisburn, Northern Ireland, I stood by my parents' grave. It was a cold, blustery, miserable winter day. Their names carved together on the headstone of their cemetery plot in Blaris Cemetery seemed surreal. I could scarcely take it in. My mind wandered back to childhood and the fears about this moment that I harbored during the early years of my life. I did not want to believe that I was seeing what was before me. Yet, there it was in gold letters carved on hard, cold, black marble. Not far from me stood a woman wearing a raincoat and plastic rain hat. She was weeping quietly. I moved in her direction to see if I might comfort her. As I drew near her she seemed oblivious to my presence. She was lost in her sorrow. As tears mingled with rain on her cheeks, I could hear her whisper, "Oh son, my son." I realized quickly that she was the mother of a young policeman murdered by terrorists. I noticed from the date on his gravestone that this was his birthday. Thirty-one years before on this very day she had given birth to him. It was a double grave. On the headstone next to his, I read the name of his father. She was a widow, too. I could begin to see why she wept as though her heart were tearing apart inside her chest. What could I say to her on a day like that? I announced my presence with a question that asked the obvious. "How are you?" She looked and tried to speak. I told her who I was. She knew my parents, she said. What could I say to comfort her? I could only remind her that God knows what it is like to have a son killed by evil men and that God's Son once stood in a cemetery and said, *"I am the resurrection, and the life: he that believeth in me, though he were dead, yet shall he live: And whosoever liveth and believeth in me shall never die"* (John 11:25,26).

WHEN THE STING IS TAKEN AWAY

"O death, where is thy sting? O grave, where is thy victory?" (1 Corinthians 15:55). Dr. Bill Iverson has been a good friend and encourager of mine. Bill's son, Danny, who was allergic to bees. In fact, Danny was so allergic to bees that a bee sting had the potential to kill him. Imagine that and put yourself in Bill's place one day when he saw a bee circling his son. Bill stood nearby and watched, afraid to get too close for fear that he would anger the bee. Finally, the bee landed on Danny, and Bill said he felt paralyzed with fear. As much as he wanted to at that very instant, Bill knew he dared not make any move toward his son. He was also afraid that Danny might attempt to swat the bee and, in the process, infuriate it. After what seemed like an eternity, the bee took off and circled around some more before it landed on Bill and swiftly stung him. Then it took off and landed on Danny again. This time, however, Bill had no fear because, unlike a wasp that can sting repeatedly, a bee can sting only once. Bill could feel the pain, but his son was safe.

Christ took death's sting in our place. Because death has lost its sting we have no need to fear it. Christ's resurrection means that we can stand in a cemetery on a miserable weather day and for a while see past the gravestones of the ones we love and have lost. Knowing the resurrected Christ, we can find somewhere deep within us—where God has placed it for such days as that—the courage to go on. What is the final answer to evil, pain, mourning, brutality, suffering, senility, sudden death, and the often mindless insanity of these times in which we live? It is that Jesus rose again from the dead and so shall we for he said so.

Mohammed's people cannot know this hope. Nor can the followers of Buddha, Confucius, or any other widely recognized world religious leaders and small g gods. All their tombs are occupied while Christ's is eternally empty. What it means is that no matter whom we follow, if we are not following Jesus, we are following a loser.

EVEN IN DEATH WE SING

J.I. Packer said, "You could speak of Jesus' rising as the most hopeful (hope-full) thing that has ever happened and you would be right."[24] Even the earliest witnesses of the faithful observed this hope. In A.D. 125, a man named Aristedes sent to an acquaintance a letter in which he attempted to explain the reasons why Christianity was spreading rapidly throughout the known world. "It is a remarkable thing to see them," he wrote. "If one of them dies, they rejoice and offer thanks to God, and they escort his body with songs and thanksgiving as if he were setting out from one place to another nearby." There is an old saying,

"Life begins at forty." For believers in Christ, however, life begins at what the world calls death. For that reason, we can face death unlike those who live with no hope.

THE IMPOSSIBILITY OF THE RESURRECTION

"Jesus of Nazareth, a man approved of God among you by miracles and wonders and signs, which God did by him in the midst of you, as ye yourselves also know: Him, being delivered by the determinate counsel and foreknowledge of God, ye have taken, and by wicked hands have crucified and slain: Whom God hath raised up, having loosed the pains of death: because it was not possible that he should be holden of it" (Acts 2:22-24).

For Jesus to lose out to death was an impossibility, Peter declared. If Jesus had not been raised from the dead, Peter, who preached these words on Pentecost Day, had no hope and no message. Instead, Peter is able to tell them that God already had his hand on the entire situation. *"Him, being delivered by the determinate counsel and foreknowledge of God, ye have taken, and by wicked hands have crucified and slain."* Peter uses the stronger of two Greek verbs to give the final lie to the hardest-headed Jew or Roman among his listeners. That word is *boule`* meaning, in effect, in this case, "When you thought you were putting Christ down for good, God had you in his hands the whole time and you simply conformed to his will." In short, Peter's choice of a Greek verb tells them that God outmaneuvered those who set about the destruction of his Son. God's enemies became his pawns. God was still in charge.

It had happened once before to Joseph, who told his brothers, *"Ye thought evil against me; but God meant it unto good" (Genesis 50:20).* God brought good out of Joseph's brothers' wicked plans, Potiphar's wife's lie, the cupbearer's forgetfulness, and seven years of famine. Joseph's experience shows us something that the Bible teaches us repeatedly. It is that God brings good out of evil for all who trust him.

He still does it. Are you trusting God enough to wait patiently while he performs his mini-resurrections in your life when the tough times come? Or, do you grow weak in the face of them? An unknown poet wrote:

Circumstances! How we pet them;
How we give them right of way!
But the Master never planned
That we should fall beneath their sway.

Paul made circumstances serve him,
Made them glorify his Lord;
Turned each trial into blessing
As he boldly preached the word.

"These things turned to my advantage,"
This old warrior oft would say.
"For our good they work together,
Though they seem to shroud the day."

It's simply true! Faith in the resurrected Jesus frees us up when life events and circumstances try to tie us down. Even when people plot evil against us, God is still on his throne. He can take the ugliest of circumstances and redeem them for something wonderful. What is it you face? Give it to him. In his time he will make it a plus factor in your life. There are mini-resurrections going on around us all through life. We've all experienced them. An old Irish saying says, "Try to drown God's man in the ocean and he'll come up with a fish in his mouth!" Because we believe in the resurrection of Jesus and because we have seen God's ability to bring amazing good out of disruption and chaos, we don't faint at circumstances. Instead, we rise above them. Because of the resurrection of Jesus, even death cannot keep us in the ground. *"Though he was crucified through weakness, yet he liveth by the power of God. For we also are weak in him, but we shall live with him by the power of God" (2 Corinthians 13:4).*

RESURRECTION EVERYDAY!

Christ's resurrection was a once-for-all-time event. He died once to take away our sins and rose again to guarantee us victory not only in heaven but also for this life. Every day we go forward in the power of the resurrection. All through life we experience pain, trials, heartbreak, temptation. *"Man that is born of a woman is of few days, and full of trouble" (Job 14:1).* Sickness, loneliness, disappointment, and the deaths of our loved ones cause us to sometimes think that life is not fair. That, in fact, is the truth. The idea that life is supposed to be fair is not founded in Scripture. Life is very unfair. There are people who suffer endlessly while others seem to know very little in the way of sorrow. Into this circumstance God brings daily mini-resurrection reflections, which, when we hear them, encourage our hearts.

Nathaniel Hawthorne, for example, lost his job to a political appointee in the Salem, Massachusetts, customhouse. It was unfair, but it happened. In the doldrums, he went home and commiserated before his wife. "Don't worry," she smiled, "at last, you will have time to focus on your book." His book, *The Scarlet Letter,* is one of American literature's masterpieces. It might have never been written had he not been terminated under hurtful circumstances.

Phillips Brooks was fired from teaching. That, too, was a dirty deal. It made him feel like a failure. Having nothing else to do, or so it seemed, he turned to the Bible. Convicted of its truth, he set his heart toward the ministry of the gospel. He became one of history's great public speakers. For more than a century now, student preachers have memorized Phillips Brooks' definition, "Preaching is truth through personality." Every Christian has sung his hymn, "O Little Town of Bethlehem." He became Episcopal bishop of Massachusetts. We would likely never have heard of him had he stayed teaching.

Perhaps only those who know failure, injustice, and hurt firsthand can truly appreciate success when it comes. Every great leader I know has experienced hurt, injustice, and a sense of personal failure. Sometimes it takes a divorce, a business failure, a public disgrace, or a big mistake to get us on course with God. For Chuck Colson it took a criminal conviction and a term in a federal penitentiary. For John Profumo it took an embarrassment that cost him a high profile government position and made him a public spectacle for months on end. He was disgraced before a nation, but he ended up as God's man doing God's work among the fallen. Failure, injustice, and hurt are often necessary parts of reaching our full potential with God. The key has always been not what we did but what we made, or are making, out of it with God's help. This is the essence of redeeming grace. What use, after all, is redeeming grace if we don't need redemption?

Our Lord said, *"Because I live, ye shall live also" (John 14:19).* C.S. Lewis writes, "A live body is not one that never gets hurt, but one that can to some extent repaid itself. In the same way a Christian is not a man who never goes wrong, but a man who is enabled to repent and pick himself up and begin over again after each stumble."[25]

Do you ever feel like a failure? Have you been treated unjustly? Has your heart been broken? The ultimate injustice happened that Friday afternoon when God's sinless Son, Jesus, hung on a cross even though he never did anything wrong. On that cross our failures were all paid in full. Through the cross our heartbreaks are guaranteed healing. God turned the cross into the world's most enduring plus sign.

"The third day he rose again from the dead." Because of that we can rise, too, and know that personal resurrection is possible for us every day. Out of our failures and heartbreaks, and that unspeakable injustice and pain brought upon his Son, God raises us up to new levels of greatness.

Coming up in the next chapter is the most practical *Life Line* of all. Read on and learn how it will bring God's blessing into your life.

CHAPTER THIRTEEN

Where Is Jesus Today?

How close is heaven to planet Earth? How far is time from eternity? Where does history connect with modernity and the future for you? And, what does it matter how we answer each of these questions? It makes a lot of difference, every day now and all through eternity. Read on and find out why.

From seven miles high on a clear day it looks like a tiny speck in the middle of the southern part of the Atlantic Ocean. We would not have noticed it had our pilot not pointed it out. Behind it lies a remarkable story of how it got its name and what its discovery meant to some ancient mariners, and the role its location has played in world history. In 1501, Portuguese mariner Juan de Nova came upon it just about the time he was wondering if he and his crew would ever see land again. It was Ascension Sunday. The captain saw it as a sign of God's deliverance and called it Ascension Island for that reason. It was on none of his maps, yet there it was, a remarkable reminder that human knowledge still had much to discover about God's amazing creation. It still does! Later, from the time of Napoleon to World War II, the island served as an important defense base for the allied forces. Its location about halfway between Africa and South America makes it an ideal spot for a re-supply center.

OUR FRIEND IN A HIGH PLACE

"I believe…He ascended into heaven and is seated at the right hand of God the Father Almighty." In a similar way, Christ's ascension provides a foundational defense and re-supply source for our spirits. Many biographies of Jesus begin in Bethlehem and end with his ascension.

His life, however, is much larger than that, and no telling of Christ's life is truly complete without reference to the consequences of his ascension. Jesus' ascension is the consummation of his redemptive work. It tells us where he is now. It explains how he can live and move in our every experience and how he will always be with us. Talk about friends in high places! They don't come any higher than this: "He ascended into heaven and is seated at the right hand of God the Father Almighty." Oswald Chambers says, "The ascension placed Jesus back in the glory which he had with the Father before the world was. The ascension, not the resurrection, is the completion of the transfiguration."

Roald Amundsen is one of the most important names in the history of polar exploration. He was the first man to discover the North Pole's magnetic meridian, to reach the South Pole, and to sail around the world via the Northwest passages. Somehow Captain Amundsen managed to navigate uncharted waters and still find time to breed homing pigeons. He carried some caged homing pigeons with him on his trips. When he reached his destination, Roald Amundsen released one of his birds. With that innate sense for which they are best known, the homing pigeon found its way back to the Amundsen home in Borge, Norway. Long before wireless communications, Mrs. Amundsen, seeing the pigeon back on its roost, knew her husband had reached his planned destination. Similarly, when Jesus ascended into heaven he was where he planned to be. His symbolic bird was not a pigeon but a dove, the Holy Spirit, who descended upon the disciples at Pentecost.

THE UNITING LIFE LINE

The *Life Line* about Jesus ascending into heaven marks that moment when the Apostles' Creed authors step out of history and into modernity. "He ascended into heaven." That is history. "And is seated at the right hand of God the Father Almighty." That is now. You might ask me where Jesus was when we were eating breakfast yesterday morning or where he is at this very minute. The answer is he was, and is, sitting at the Father's right hand. This is where theology becomes more than a system of belief. It becomes undeniably practical. What I believe about Christ's present whereabouts changes everything about my view of life and gives me a pattern for living that is foundationally richer than the belief systems of the followers of all the small g gods in history. It brings heaven and Earth together as nothing else. It connects time with eternity, and joins history with modernity and the future for all our lives. It gives us an answer they do not have when life deals us ugly blows. Jesus, who died for me and rose again, now lives for me with the Father! With Job, we can say in the midst of tough times, *"I know that my redeemer liveth" (Job 19:25).*

"Where is your Jesus when little children starve to death in Somalia?" Although that question came to me from a pure skeptic, it is a good one. I commended him for his sensitivity and added to his inquiry a few questions others in a similar frame of mind have asked: "Where is he when a baby dies at Children's Hospital of Pittsburgh? Or, when cancer strikes? Or, when downsizing brings about financial ruin? Or, when an airplane crashes into the ocean killing everyone on board? Where was he when a little girl was discovered brutally murdered in her own home on Christmas Day?"

THE BEST PLACE FOR JESUS

These are the kinds of questions reasonable people ask. The answer to all these, and like questions, is that Jesus sits at the Father's right hand where *"he ever liveth to make intercession for them" (Hebrews 7:25)*. In short, Christ is where we need him most of all when difficult circumstances enter our lives. He is in the Father's presence pleading our case for *"we have not an high priest which cannot be touched with the feeling of our infirmities" (Hebrews 4:15)*. As tough as life can be, it would be tougher were Christ not there. Because he is there we live with the comfort of knowing he has our loved ones in safe care. He understands their needs.

SYMPATHY VERSUS EMPATHY

A dog fancier advertised puppies for sale with a sign in a local store window. Among the respondents was a little boy. "How much are they?" the youngster asked the man. "They cost $150 each," the man replied. "All I have is $1.15," the lad replied. "Could I even look at them for that?" "Sure," the owner said, smiling. The little fellow looked down into the cage where the puppies played. He noticed that one of them was not playing. It was smaller than the others. It had a deformed leg that made walking more difficult. Compared to the others, it moved awkwardly. "What happened to that one?" he asked the owner. "It was born like that," the owner said, "and the vet says there's not much we can do to straighten that leg out. I'm afraid the poor little thing will always be crippled." "I'd like to buy that one," said the boy. "Could I make a down payment of $1.15 and pay off the rest when I get the money?" he asked. The dogs' owner smiled. "Why would you want it, son? You know, the vet says it'll always be small, always have a limp and won't be able to run and play as well as the others." As the man spoke, the lad raised his trouser leg just enough to reveal a brace that ran down each side of his leg and was attached to a specially manufactured shoe. He said, "That's exactly why I want it, mister. 'Cause I don't run so good myself and I figure it's gonna need somebody who understands it." That youngster's own experience provided him with just the kind of compassion that puppy needed. Where others could sympathize with "the poor little thing," he could empathize.

The ascended Christ understands, out of his personal experience, when evil people break into our lives and destroy something precious. He knows about it firsthand. He comprehends suffering as one who suffered. He knows all about a young life cut off at the dawn of a promising future because vicious killers ended his own life at its peak. He weeps for the sin that often brings about devastation and human tragedy, and he waits in heaven to greet its victims with identifying empathy. When they enter the Father's house, he is always there to greet them. He understands, he cares, and he is in the best possible place he can be to represent us. At his ascension Christ entered heaven where he makes sure the door stays open for our arrival. Can you think of a better place for him to be? Or, a place where you would rather he would be? Can you think of any other religion whose leader offers personal care in the Father's throne room?

WHERE PHILOSOPHY AND PRACTICALITY MEET

"Unto every one of us is given grace according to the measure of the gift of Christ. Wherefore he saith, When he ascended up on high, he led captivity captive, and gave gifts unto men. (Now that he ascended, what is it but that he also descended first into the lower parts of the earth? He that descended is the same also that ascended up far above all heavens, that he might fill all things.) And he gave some, apostles; and some, prophets; and some, evangelists; and some, pastors and teachers; For the perfecting of the saints, for the work of the ministry, for the edifying of the body of Christ" (Ephesians 4:7-12).

Now we get into something else that is unique to followers of the ascended Jesus. It is the amazing practicality of his gospel. This Christ we follow is no pie-in-the-sky-when-you-die-by-and-by religious philosopher. What he passes on to us and what he asks us to pass along to others is the most practical system of belief the world will ever know. How practical is the message of the ascended Jesus? If, somehow, it were possible to extract Christ out of the gospel and leave only his teachings, it would still be the most workable set of life lessons ever devised. That is why so many of the so-called "self-help" systems offered in the marketplace quote him often. If we dissect the teachings of the more successful ones, we soon realize that what they teach is actually what Christ taught first. Through the clever use of synonyms, others often market his philosophies as their own.

SHOE LEATHER RELIGION

This is a transitional phrase in the Creed for yet another reason. Not only does it join history to modernity and the future, it joins the philosophy of theology (often called "theology proper") to practical theology. Moreover, in doing that it challenges a thinking person to see and apply the practical responsibilities of being a Christian.

Jesus *"went about doing good" (Acts 10:38)*. Near the old center of Birmingham, Alabama, a statue is erected to honor the memory of Brother Brian of Birmingham. Brother Brian touched the lives of untold numbers of people because he practiced his gospel. For him, theology was more than a system of belief. It was a way of life. Therefore, his statue bears the appropriate inscription "Religion in Shoes." Christianity has been called the "shoe leather religion" because it calls the blessed to go to the less blessed and bless them in Jesus' name. This has historically been true throughout our history. Wherever Christ's missionaries have traveled, they have left hospitals, schools, and churches that in Jesus' name have served to advance the good of people in those regions.

When the Olympic torch was making its way from Athens, Greece, to Atlanta, Georgia, for the Centennial Olympic games, a friend of ours was selected to carry the torch for one mile through north Georgia. Someone asked him, "What are you supposed to do with it?" He replied, "I'm supposed to run with it as hard as I can and pass it along to somebody else." When Christ ascended, he passed his gospel torch into our hands. He wants you and me to run with it as fast as we can and pass it along to others.

Someone has let his imagination picture an apocryphal scene when Jesus entered heaven immediately following his ascension. The angels celebrated the success of their Master's earthly mission. As they chatted enthusiastically together, first one and then another started vying for their teacher's favor. Each of them wanted to be chosen before all the others to carry God's new good news to planet Earth. It was a story worth telling. They could imagine their potential audience held in rapt attention. They could imagine the joy it would bring to everyone who heard that human shame and guilt were wiped away at Calvary. Finally, one particularly excited angel could wait no longer and blurted out, "Who will it be, Master? Who will be first to tell your story?" Jesus smiled back toward Earth and singled out the little band of followers he had left behind only minutes before. "There they are," he declared. "They are my witnesses. They will tell my story to the world. My light will shine wherever they carry it."

That torch of the gospel that first was lighted at Jerusalem and handed to the church has been carried through generations and across oceans and continents. It was passed to us by whoever told us his story. Now we hold it. We will determine what future, if any, it has. We will decide how far it will be carried in this generation. The reality of the ascension is this: We in the church have a job to do as Christ's primary representatives on Earth. *"Seeing we also are compassed about with so great a cloud of witnesses, let us lay aside every weight, and the sin which doth so easily beset us, and let us run with patience the race that is set before us, Looking unto Jesus the author and finisher of our faith; who for the joy that was set before him endured the cross, despising the shame, and is set down at the right hand of the throne of God"* (Hebrews 12:1,2).

EARTH MEETS HEAVEN

"In my Father's house are many mansions: if it were not so, I would have told you. I go to prepare a place for you. And if I go and prepare a place for you, I will come again, and receive you unto myself; that where I am, there ye may be also...I am the way, the truth, and the life: no man cometh unto the Father, but by me" (John 14:2,3,6). The everlasting Christ, who now lives beyond time as we know it, accomplished his earthly mission. Now he has a heavenly assignment. It is to prepare a place for us among the Father's mansions. Time and eternity, heaven and earth, mortality and immortality are thus co-joined because of his ascension. In his ascent, our ascent is guaranteed.

In the last chapter and the one before it we saw that Christ on Calvary took death's sting away. Yet, that is not all he did for us. He ascended to prepare our place in the Father's house.

RUTH'S REALITY

Ruth Davis was one of the first women to be licensed to practice law by the State of Georgia. She spent significant time each week writing notes and letters to a number of people. Ruth was one of the most encouraging Christians I have known. A number of her letters are preserved carefully in a special file in my office. When Ruth was diagnosed with a form of cancer that her physicians said would spread rapidly and take her life in a relatively short period of time, many of us were alarmed. None of us likes to say goodbye to special friends, even though they may be elderly, and even for a little while. Sensing something of my dismay, Ruth wrote me a remarkable letter. In it she said, "My doctors, who are all good friends, tell me I will die soon. Don't you believe a word of it! I'm going to be more alive than ever. Would you like to know where I will be? I will be in my Father's house, in a mansion Jesus has prepared for me there. I will be where I want to be. In fact, I will be exactly where I have been looking forward to being for a long time now. Would you like to know how it will be for me there? I will be perfect in every way. Would you like to know what I will be doing there? I will be looking into the face of my Redeemer. Just imagine, I, who could never carry a tune before, will be singing in his choir! Would you like to know who will be with me there? The best people that ever walked on earth. Among them will be many of my old friends with whom I practiced and prayed over the years. Of course, I hope that one day you will be there, too. Would you like to know how long I expect to stay there? I expect to be there until the nightfall of a day that has no sunset. In other words, I'll be there forever. Isn't this wonderful? Please don't weep for me." She signed it, "Lovingly your friend, Ruth."

How could Ruth Davis and thousands of Christians like her face death with such grace and equanimity? Only because of the ascension of Jesus, her Lord! Her heart was not troubled for she believed what he said. Because of that belief, heaven was just as sure for her as the ground she walked on here on Earth each day. Earth and heaven met for Ruth, and for all who believe in him, when she saw the resurrected and ascended Christ face-to-face for the first time. Time and eternity melded as one.

Do you believe "He ascended into heaven and is seated at the right hand of God the Father Almighty?" If you do, every word in Ruth's letter can be written over your signature, too. Perhaps you even need to write a letter like that to someone you love. All the promises Ruth anticipated being filled when she arrived in heaven will be filled for you too because of Jesus. If you have not made a commitment to trust Christ for his heaven, there will never be a better time than this. Why not, before you read another page, surrender your life to him now?

Perhaps someone reading these words asks how to do this. The answer is through repentance and faith. That means acknowledging your sins and asking Christ to forgive them. After that, ask him to come into your heart and guide your life from now on. When you do that and believe it, you will come through time to know Ruth Davis' confidence in Christ's finished atonement.

HIS LIFE THROUGH US

"Why stand ye gazing up into heaven? This same Jesus, which is taken up from you into heaven, shall so come in like manner as ye have seen him go into heaven" (Acts 1:11). The final link of this *Life Line* brings together belief and action, intellectual assent and deeds. It is not enough to merely profess belief in Christ's ascension with our lips. We must demonstrate it with our lives. When we least expect it, the clouds that once received

Christ will break open to reveal him again. The ascended Master will return. It could even be today!

If Christ does come today, what will he find you doing to advance his work on Earth? Are you doing all you can for him with all he has made you and all he has given you?

During World War I, a talented young concert pianist was drafted and sent to the front line of the battlefield. His right arm was badly mangled in a fierce battle. Medics, recognizing that death was imminent unless they amputated that arm, cut it off. Although devastated, the young pianist determined that battlefield surgery would not hinder his dreams of playing around the world. He was discharged and sent home. The young pianist began a new campaign. It was, in some ways, even harder than the campaign he had been through on the battlefront. He traipsed from composer to composer asking for any piano arrangements they might have written for the left hand only. One by one they sympathized and politely turned him away. He seemed to get nowhere but determined not to give up. Finally, he visited Maurice Ravel, the brilliant French composer of *Bolero*. Maurice Ravel felt empathy when he observed the young man's courage. The great Ravel resolved to write a concerto especially for his newfound, determined friend. The *Ravel Concerto in D Major for Left Hand* was composed. For years after it was written, audiences were packed into many of Europe's finest and largest concert halls to hear it played by that young man with only one arm. As they watched him and listened to his music, they became stirred with new passion. That young pianist played all across Europe and the United States. He could not play any two-handed concertos, but he could surely play this one with all his heart.

What is your handicap? See it as an opportunity to rise above it in Christ. Take it in stride and go after your best dreams with passion. There is no telling where God, through the ascended Christ's Spirit, will take you.

The Second Coming of Jesus Christ is nearer than it ever was before. Many Bible scholars agree he might come at any time. *"The Son of man cometh at an hour when ye think not" (Luke 12:40)*. His coming is the subject of the next chapter. Before you turn the page, resolve that with Christ's help you will play your part with passion. Don't stand around looking up. There is a time and place where heaven and Earth come together. Why not resolve to make that place where you are and that time now?

GET READY TO GO UP

Jesus was not the first to ascend. Elijah went before him: *"Behold, there appeared a chariot of fire, and horses of fire, and parted them both asunder; and Elijah went up by a whirlwind into heaven" (2 Kings 2:11)*.

Even before that, Enoch, who *"walked with God: and he was not; for God took him" (Genesis 5:24),* ascended. Little Cameron listened intently as her Sunday school teacher told her Enoch's story. On the way home from church, her Mom asked her what she had learned. She gushed, "Mommy, you wouldn't believe it. My teacher told us about a man who went out for a walk with God every day. One day they walked and walked and walked till it was almost dark. And when the man started to go back, the Lord said to him, 'Enoch, you've walked with me so long, why don't you just come home to my house and play?'"

"The Lord himself shall descend from heaven with a shout, with the voice of the archangel, and with the trump of God: and the dead in Christ shall rise first: Then we which are alive and remain shall be caught up together with them in the clouds, to meet the Lord in the air: and so shall we ever be with the Lord" (1 Thessalonians 4:16,17). One day, in one form or another, we also shall ascend. To borrow Cameron's words, one day Christ will say to us, "Why don't you just come home to my house?" On that day, time and eternity will meet, heaven and Earth will be bridged, mortality and immortality become one, and the best place for Jesus will become the best place for us. In the meantime, we can live every day with confidence knowing that the One who loved us all the way to Calvary meets daily with the Father on our behalf.

In the next chapter, we will explore the one amazing event for which the whole creation groans and meet a judge no king can own and no money can buy.

CHAPTER FOURTEEN

Will Jesus Christ Come Back to Earth?

Is there more to life than meets the eye? Is history being directed? Or, does it merely happen by random chance? Is there a central amazing event toward which this universe is soaring? If so, what is it? How can we prepare for it? In this chapter, you will meet a judge no king can own and no money can buy. Read on.

Atop the Capitol dome in Washington, D.C., an inscription that few tourists ever see speaks to the consummation of history as we know it. It reads, "One far-off divine event toward which the whole creation moves." It describes the all-consuming event toward which this universe is soaring, *"That blessed hope, and the glorious appearing of the great God and our Saviour Jesus Christ" (Titus 2:13).* The Creed authors declared, "Jesus Christ shall come again to judge the living and the dead." Do you believe it?

NOT THE END

More than a century ago, an English nobleman fell seriously ill. His physician was called to examine him and came to a conclusion neither of them wanted to hear: "I fear, Sir, that you are going to die." Without a thought, the nobleman replied, "Die, dear Doctor? Why that's the last thing I intend to do!" In reality, dying is not the last thing any of us will do. The Bible says, *"It is appointed unto men once to die, but after this the judgment" (Hebrews 9:27).*

For the most part, our Elijah generation with its plethora of small g gods, seems to ignore this central mile marker that no one can avoid.

119

We will not all die. Yet, even for those of us who do die, death will not be the last thing we do. After we die, there will be a judgment.

Unlike prior generations of Americans and Western Europeans, we seem to have abandoned any notion of a polestar by which we might set our life's compass and chart our national courses. It's a time when anything goes. Solomon reminds us, *"Where there is no vision, the people perish" (Proverbs 29:18)*. The *New King James Version* of the Bible translates this sentence, *"Where there is no revelation, the people cast off restraint."* The Hebrew is, in fact, saying that when people have no clear sense of right and wrong they run amok. History proves it. Where there is ignorance of God and his word, crime rates soar and human decency declines. When a nation of people raises a generation without full reference to the gospel, that nation begins a downward moral spiral. Its young people become unguided and hopeless. In that sense, we can see why suicide is at epidemic rates among people under thirty all across the western world. The message of the university, and sometimes the church, seems to be that there are no firm standards; no absolutes by which to measure our lives; nor rules against which we will be measured. The prime example of that, in our time, is the self-inflicted agonizing struggle that many United States mainline denominations are putting themselves through in their efforts to accommodate moral and ethical behavior patterns that frequently run in direct opposition to the plain teachings of Scripture. They are being sideswiped by unbelief and doubt, and appear to have neither the energy nor the commitment to truth to respond in a way that honors the Lord of the church. Can you remember the last time you heard a sermon on the final judgment in your church?

THE FIRST LAW OF HARVEST

An ancient legend tells about a farmhand who was instructed to plant barley in a field. He went to work and all seemed well. However, one afternoon some weeks later the farmer walked out to his field. Upon observing his crop, he realized that instead of barley he was growing oats. The farmer was furious. He hastily summoned the farmhand to meet him at the barn. When the two were face to face, the enraged boss declared, "I said plant barley, but all I see growing is oats. Why did you not do what you were told?" "Because I didn't think it would make any difference," the farmhand replied. By this time, the farmer was livid. "Are you so stupid, man," he yelled, "that you don't know that planting oats will produce oats and planting barley will produce barley?" "Actually, boss," the laborer told the farmer, "I got the idea from you. I've observed how you live. You frequently sow wild oats but tell folks about your righteous expectations." The farmer's hypocrisy was being watched even when he did not realize it. His actions were so deafening they drowned out his words.

We are being watched, too. *"Whatsoever a man soweth, that shall he also reap" (Galatians 6:7)*. This is the first law of harvest. There are unavoidable natural consequences to how we live. There are standards that cannot be dodged. There are harvests that shall be reaped and events that will impact our lives, even if we choose not to believe in them.

We reap what we sow. Nothing we can do will change that. All our efforts to scrap the Bible's message about future history and God's judgment on persistent sin will not make it go away. God's sovereign intention for the universe will not pale because we disregard his word.

What is more, when we downplay this part of the Christian message to the world, we deprive people of the *"blessed hope"* that life will finally make sense, that its puzzles have answers, and that divine justice works. To believe other than this is to ignore the obvious and make chance the director of our lives. What tragedy we birth when we allow that to happen!

We are not the first to disregard this part of God's message. Elijah's generation found such a belief system initially unappealing, too. It seems, on the surface, to be harsh. We should not be surprised that it is a life philosophy still unpopular with many people.

A true story, told to me by a minister friend, speaks of one elderly fellow who claimed he enjoyed good preaching and studying the Bible. However, despite his declaration, he was a tyrant at home. His pastor observed this behavior and warned him of the consequences. Nothing changed. Finally, in desperation the minister cautioned, "If you persist in such conduct you will end up a lonely, unloved old man. One day, your family will reach their tolerance limits and your friends will simply stop coming by to visit you." The old man paid no heed. His behavior continued and grew worse with time's passing. The man's wife, fearing for her own safety, was forced to leave home soon after that conversation. His children found him unbearable and effectively disowned him. Friends, who once had demonstrated remarkable patience with his gruff arrogance, stopped visiting. He did, in fact, spend his last years as a lonely, rejected, and miserable man.

HARD OF LISTENING

In a corporate sense there is an example of that in the Bible. Ezekiel's generation listened to his impassioned preaching about finding new life through obeying God's decrees. They heard Ezekiel's voice, yet failed to heed his message. They were not hard of hearing. They were hard of listening. Their old sinful behavior patterns continued unabated. Alas,

121

as Ezekiel warned, the Babylonians came. Only in captivity in Babylon did the Israelites awaken to the error of hearing God's word but not heeding it. It was too late. Judgment came to God's people. They were not exempt because they were his. It is a perilous thing to know God's will and not follow it.

OUR NORTH STAR

Jesus "Shall come again," declared the authors of the Apostles' Creed. Will we believe and heed it? His coming is the North Star by which history is guided to its close. On a personal level, he is the unmovable and unchangeable reality whose word is the compass and handbook through which we can steer the ship of our lives in preparation for that "one far-off divine event." Are you making ready for Christ's Second Coming?

DOING DIFFERENTLY

An Irish wit once declared, "Live every day as though it will be your last and one day you will be right!" Behind that sense of humor lies unalterable wisdom. It can also be said, "Live every day as though Christ is coming and one day you will be right." If you knew that today was your last day on Earth, is there anything you would do differently? Are there lifestyle changes you would make if you knew that this is the day of Christ's return? Is there a telephone call you would hurriedly make? A letter you would rush to write? If there is, let me encourage you to do it today. Is there someone you need to thank for giving you a chance that set your life in the right direction? Thank that person today. Drop a note, pay a visit, make a phone call. The stage is set for Christ's coming. He could return before you finish reading this chapter. Maybe you should set this book down while you accomplish what is necessary.

NEW PRIORITIES

When she knew she was dying, Erma Bombeck, America's first lady of humor, wrote her readers a personal column entitled "If I Had My Life to Live Over." Here is some of what she said she would do differently:

"I would have burned the pink candle sculpted like a rose before it melted in storage."

"I would have talked less and listened more."

"There would have been more 'I love yous' and more 'I'm sorrys.'"

"When my kids kissed me impetuously, I would have never said, 'Later, now go get washed up for dinner!'"

"Don't worry about who doesn't like you, who has more, or who's doing what. Instead let's cherish the relationships we have with those who DO love us. Let's think about what God HAS blessed us with. And, what we're doing each day to promote ourselves mentally, physically, emotionally, as well as spiritually. Life is too short to let it pass you by. We have only one shot at this and then it's gone."

What might you write in her situation? Why not write it out, send it to someone you love, and determine to make it an action plan for how you will live the rest of your life?

Erma Bombeck's priorities were transformed by her recognition of life's brevity. Perhaps the time has come for yours to be transformed, too.

CLOSER THAN YOU THINK!

"The immense step from Babe at Bethlehem to the living reigning triumphant Lord Jesus, returning to earth for his own people—that is the glorious truth proclaimed throughout Scripture."[26] The return is a colossal distance from the Bethlehem manger, but it may be mere seconds away from us. Have you ever thought about why your car's passenger side door mirror has a warning that "objects in mirror are closer than they appear"? It is because the mirror on the passenger side of almost all American cars is convex to allow for a wider angle of vision. We can rephrase some of those words and say with certainty that Christ's Second Coming is closer now than it has ever been at any time in history. While the Bible clearly says we do not, and cannot, know when that "one far-off divine event toward which the whole creation moves" will be, we can say with certainty that the passing of the years draws us ever nearer to the time when the Lord will return. The clouds may break at any moment and Christ will reappear. Whether now or later, we can say with confidence, "He will come again." Let us resolve to make this the guiding principle for our lives.

PRO MILLENNIALISM

The Creed does not discuss the fine details of the Second Coming. It simply affirms that Jesus will return. I recall a seminary discussion on this issue. The merits and demerits of each millennial view were being enthusiastically debated by a group of heady seminary students. The millennial views each set forth the scenario for Christ's Second Coming. Temper temperatures were showing signs of rising when a common-sense fellow interjected, "When it comes to millennial positions, I'm pro-mill!" "What do you mean?" a debate leader asked. "I mean that no matter how the Lord chooses to come, I'm going to be in favor of it." His is a prudent position to take. It might even be the implied position of the Creed authors since they identify no other. This we know: Next to salvation by grace through faith, the Second Coming of Jesus is the best-attested fact of the New Testament.

From start to finish the Bible addresses the fact of Christ's return. Some New Testament scholars reckon that one verse in every thirteen speaks to this "one far-off divine event toward which the whole creation moves." It is a clear and present reality.

THE JUDGE NO KING CAN OWN

The Creed authors also give the reason for the Lord's return: "He will come to judge the living and the dead." Exactly what does Christ's judgment entail? Who better to answer that question for us than Jesus?

"When the Son of man shall come in his glory, and all the holy angels with him, then shall he sit upon the throne of his glory: And before him shall be gathered all nations: and he shall separate them one from another, as a shepherd divideth his sheep from the goats: And he shall set the sheep on his right hand, but the goats on the left. Then shall the King say unto them on his right hand, 'Come, ye blessed of my Father, inherit the kingdom prepared for you from the foundation of the world: For I was an hungered, and ye gave me meat: I was thirsty, and ye gave me drink: I was a stranger, and ye took me in: Naked, and ye clothed me: I was sick, and ye visited me: I was in prison, and ye came unto me.' Then shall the righteous answer him, saying, 'Lord, when saw we thee an hungered, and fed thee? or thirsty, and gave thee drink? When saw we thee a stranger, and took thee in? or naked, and clothed thee? Or when saw we thee sick, or in prison, and came unto thee?' And the King shall answer and say unto them, 'Verily I say unto you, Inasmuch as ye have done it unto one of the least of these my brethren, ye have done it unto me.' Then shall he say also unto them on the left hand, 'Depart from me, ye cursed, into everlasting fire, prepared for the devil and his angels: For I was an hungered, and ye gave me no meat: I was thirsty, and ye gave me no drink: I was a stranger, and ye took me not in: naked, and ye clothed me not: sick, and in prison, and ye visited me not.' Then shall they also answer him, saying, Lord, when saw we thee an hungered, or athirst, or a stranger, or naked, or sick, or in prison, and did not minister unto thee? Then shall he answer them, saying, 'Verily I say unto you, Inasmuch as ye did it not to one of the least of these, ye did it not to me. And these shall go away into everlasting punishment: but the righteous into life eternal'" (Matthew 25:31-46).

THE MAN OUTSIDE THE DOOR

In sentences composed to afflict the comfortable and comfort the afflicted, Jesus leaves very little to our imaginations. He says he will separate true believers from phonies and the difference between the two will be not in what is professed, but in what is done.

An unknown person writes:

It was a cold winter's day that Sunday. The church parking lot was filling up quickly. As I left my car, I noticed several groups of church members huddling together and apparently whispering to each other as they made their way to church. Soon, I saw the reason why, or thought I did. It was the figure of a man leaning up against the wall outside the church door. He could have been asleep. His long trench coat was dirty and obviously had seen better days, much better! His hat was pulled down to protect his face from the icy morning air. What little of his countenance I saw looked rough. Obviously he had not shaved in some days. The bottoms of his trouser legs were observably turned up several times, indicating they had once belonged to a much taller man. They, too, were dirty and looked threadbare. The shoes below them were hardly worthy of the name. They looked ancient and they were far too small for his feet. One had a hole in front so that part of his big toe peered out. I was struck by the fact that he seemed to be wearing no socks on this freezing cold morning. He was just another street bum, I thought. I steered wide of him as I made my way into our new sanctuary. Once inside, I removed my heavy winter coat and the sports coat I was wearing underneath it. I hung them with my scarf, my hat and my gloves and made my way inside the cozy sanctuary and greeted some of my church friends. We welcomed each other warmly and fellowshipped for a few minutes over coffee and donuts. Someone mentioned the tramp outside the door. Someone else responded by making a joke about him. A few of us laughed but our laughter was cut short when we observed him half-walk, half-hobble into the sanctuary. He held onto the walls for support as he edged slowly along. His hat was still on and his head was down. Didn't he know to remove his hat in church? People peered at him then quickly tried to ignore him. When he approached the coffee urn, people nearby moved nearer to each other in an effort not to be too close to him. As he moved past them, some members of the congregation whispered. A few made faces and one or two gasped in horror. He ambled slowly towards the front of the sanctuary. "Where in the world is the pastor when we need him?" somebody asked impatiently. The man from outside dragged his feet up the three steps into our pulpit. A couple of the bigger fellows could take no more and moved in to move him out. It was too late. He proceeded to undress right there, before us all. Off came the raunchy overcoat and the dirty, greasy hat. He reached inside his torn trousers for a towel and began to wipe his face. His head was still down as he ran his hand through his hair like a five fingered comb. Then he looked up at us and we all stopped suddenly in our tracks, unable to believe what we were seeing. The praise team, that, moments before, was finishing up its rehearsal for the morning service went silent. The trumpet player lowered his horn in unbelief and gasped, "Where in the world is the pastor when we need him?" Suddenly he realized this outsider was our pastor. He was made up to look like a homeless person. He smiled and said, "Hi, folks! I don't have a sermon today but I do have a text. Here it is straight from the Master: *"'Verily I say unto you, Inasmuch as ye did it not to one of the least of these, ye did it not to me.'"* Having read the Scripture, he began to sing a chorus: *"If I can help somebody as I pass along; If I can cheer somebody with a word or song; If I can show somebody that he's traveling wrong; Then my living will not be in vain."*

In Matthew 25:31-46, Jesus, who "will come to judge the living and the dead," provides a checklist of assignments so simple a child can understand them. They need no exegesis from a heady theologian. They require no wealth, no supernatural ability, and nothing but average intelligence to accomplish. They are simple acts of grace to be done in his name. They leave room for neither neglect nor excuse. In short, the Lord of the church and of every Christian demands our personal involvement in caring for folks like the man outside the door.

"Cry aloud, spare not, lift up thy voice like a trumpet, and show my people their transgression, and the house of Jacob their sins. Yet they seek me daily, and delight to know my ways, as a nation that did righteousness, and forsook not the ordinance of their God: they ask of me the ordinances of justice; they take delight in approaching to God. Wherefore have we fasted, say they, and thou seest not? Wherefore have we afflicted our soul, and thou takest no knowledge? Behold, in the day of your fast ye find pleasure, and exact all your labours. Behold, ye fast for strife and debate, and to smite with the fist of wickedness: ye shall not fast as ye do this day, to make your voice to be heard on high. Is it such a fast that I have chosen? A day for a man to afflict his soul? Is it to bow down his head as a bulrush, and to spread sackcloth and ashes under him? Wilt thou call this a fast, and an acceptable day to the LORD? Is not this the fast that I have chose, to loose the bands of wickedness, to undo the heavy burdens, and to let the oppressed go free, and that ye break every yoke? Is it not to deal thy bread to the hungry, and that thou bring the poor that are cast out to thy house? When

126

thou seest the naked, that thou cover him; and that thou hide not thyself from thine own flesh? Then shall thy light break forth as the morning, and thine health shall spring forth speedily: and thy righteousness shall go before thee; the glory of the LORD shall be thy rereward" (Isaiah 58:1-8).

"He shall come again to judge the living and the dead." Think about it and do these things!

What do we believe? We believe what we do! Not what we say! History is being directed in ways that provide daily opportunities to declare our beliefs to the world. How can we prepare for Christ's coming judgment? Simply by obeying his commandments. Christ will come as a judge no king can own and no money can buy.

"Watch ye therefore: for ye know not when the master of the house cometh, at even, or at midnight, or at the cockcrowing, or in the morning: Lest coming suddenly he find you sleeping. And what I say unto you I say unto all, 'Watch'" (Mark 13:35-37).

The next chapter introduces us to the most powerful person in the world today. Read on and be encouraged to live your life on a higher plane than ever before.

CHAPTER FIFTEEN

Who Is the Most Powerful Person in the World Today?

Who is this "most powerful person in the world today" that I mentioned in the closing paragraph of the previous chapter? Is this a man or a woman? Could it be the head of the United Nations or the European Economic Council? Is the president of the United States the one? Is it a leader in the world of business and commerce, perhaps one who spearheads the information revolution? Could it be Bill Gates? The Sultan of Oman? Or, is this someone you know? Should I really ask, "What is it?" Are we speaking not of a person but an impersonal force? In this chapter, we will find the answer to each of these questions and discover extraordinary power for living. Read on and allow your mind and heart to soar to new levels.

When he was born, his parents named him Edson Arantes do Nascimento. When he played, his fans nicknamed him "Perola Negra," or "Black Pearl." When he ran faster than they could shout those words to cheer him on, they simply shortened his nickname to Pele. An average-sized man, his speed, balance, vision, and ability to control a ball are legend to soccer fans on every continent. Like no other man before or since, his feet brought life to a pair of stiff, leather soccer boots. Someone wrote that when Pele put his feet into them, his boots came to life. As Pele's feet brought life to a pair of soccer boots, so there is someone who can enter our lives and bring life to us.

"I believe in the Holy Spirit." When I declare this *Life Line* with our church family each Sunday, I am all too aware that no part of the Godhead is more misunderstood, maligned, or understated than the Spirit of God. Some have relegated him to unwanted stepchild status in God's family. They acknowledge his presence but would be just as happy if he would keep himself quiet and out of sight. Others go to the opposite extreme, treating him like an old-time snake oil salesman's favorite potent product. Neither of these images is based on the Bible's verbal portrait of him. They are mere figments of imagination and misunderstanding.

OUR COMFORTER

"I will pray the Father, and he shall give you another Comforter, that he may abide with you for ever; Even the Spirit of truth; whom the world cannot receive, because it seeth him not, neither knoweth him: but ye know him; for he dwelleth with you, and shall be in you" (John 14:16,17).

Jesus, about to leave his first disciples, assures them that although he will no longer be seen in their company, he will still be present with them in the form of *"another Comforter."* The Greek word for *"Comforter"* is *parakletos,* a compound of two other Greek words. The first, *para,* means one who supports, helps, and encourages. It forms the front end of some English words commonly used in our society. A paramedic, for example, supports medical doctors. A paralegal helps lawyers with legal issues. The second part of the word for *"Comforter"* is from the Greek root *kaleo,* meaning call. Our English word "call" is a direct phonetic derivative of *kaleo.* When we join *para* to *kletos* we have *parakletos,* meaning someone who assists or helps us because that is their calling. The *Comforter* Jesus promised is the Holy Spirit.

THE ULTIMATE OVERSEER

Since before history began, the Holy Spirit has assumed special roles as part of the Trinity. He helped shape creation. *"The earth was without form, and void; and darkness was upon the face of the deep. And the Spirit of God moved upon the face of the waters" (Genesis 1:2).* Just as a building superintendent would oversee a gigantic construction project in any of the world's great cities, so God's Holy Spirit would have given oversight to the formation of the universe. He determined the shape and size of the planets and continents. He carved the contours of the mountains and hills, and determined the direction of the flow of the oceans.

As part of the creation process, he gave life to the first man: *"The LORD God formed man of the dust of the ground, and breathed into his nostrils the breath of life; and man became a living soul." (Genesis 2:7).* His is the breath of eternal life that makes us different from all other species. It not only makes us live, it kindles a yearning within us for fellowship with God that is resident in nothing else we know. We are spiritual beings, made for communion with our Creator. Until we find that, the elevator of life never reaches the top floor of existence. [27]

This same Holy Spirit supervised the writing of the Scriptures. He caused the Bible to be penned in words we can understand and relate to life today. What is more, he stamps the authority of the eternal God upon its words: *"All scripture is given by inspiration of God" (2 Timothy 3:16).* Paul coins a compound word from *theos,* meaning *"God,"* and *pneuma,* meaning *"breathe."* The Bible is God's breath. The Spirit is also the breath of God. His name in Greek is *"hagios pneuma,"* meaning *"the holy breath."* So, when we read that God breathes out Scripture, we can conclude that the Holy Breath of God carried out that process. *"This scripture must needs have been fulfilled, which the Holy Ghost by the mouth of David spake before" (Acts 1:16).* Who wrote David's psalms? Was it David? Yes, but the Holy Spirit breathed the words into David's heart, just as he did to all the writers of the Bible.

SUPERVISOR OF THE SEASONS

The same Holy Spirit works today. He breathes life into our deadness and hope into our hopelessness. He breathes healing on our broken hearts and on all that lives around us: *"Thou sendest forth thy spirit, they are created: and thou renewest the face of the earth" (Psalm 104:30).* As I write these words, the tree outside my study window is waking after a winter of sleep. Tiny green leaves are breaking out all across branches that just a few days ago were purely brown. Across the street, daffodils are blooming. To the uninitiated they announce that spring is back in Pittsburgh. To believers they signal that the Holy Spirit is *"renewing the face of the earth."* He still supervises the seasons.

He also supervises the seasons of our lives. When we feel down, God's Spirit comes to redirect our thinking and renew us. He arrests us on the road to ruin and redirects us toward renewal and hope. He reminds us God loves us and draws us to remember our salvation. He seals our relationship with Christ. He empowers us to accomplish greater things than we have imagined and to reach for new goals. He is our friend *"that sticketh closer than a brother"* for as long as we live (see *Proverbs 18:24*). He always looks out for what is best for us. He is without a doubt the most powerful person in the world today. Without the Holy Spirit, it is impossible to achieve the positive life change Christ promises and we need.

POWER PLUS PERSONALITY

What is he really like? To begin to understand the answer to this question, we must first settle a foundational understanding about the one who is the theme of this chapter. The mother of two little girls defined the essential difference between her daughters to me not long ago: "This one will succeed on power and that one through personality," she said. It was a mom's humorous one-sentence analysis of her children's different strengths and abilities. One is brainy. The other is cute. One is pushy, always wanting to lead. The other tries to please and is willing to compromise and share. One is a high achiever on all the standardized tests. The other doesn't do so well but has a smile that would melt a heart of steel. One makes straight As in school without ever seeming to study. The other works hard just to make Bs. One is powerful. She is calculating and survives through her brainpower. The other is a real personality. She is warm and loving and survives by winning hearts.

Power and personality! Sometimes the difference between two people can be defined using those words. Each of us is gifted with a heavier dose of one or the other of these two qualities. Observe someone function for a while and one inevitably dominates the other.

Consider two leaders whose names will be recorded in twentieth century history. What made Winston Churchill the dynamic leader he was for the European allies during the Second World War? It was not overwhelming intelligence. Churchill was not stupid but he never demonstrated better-than-average brainpower in his entire academic life. It was his personality that made him a leader. He drew people together through who he was rather than by what he was. When he said to the British people at the outset of the bombings, "I have nothing to offer you but blood, sweat and tears," they listened to his voice and made ready to bleed, sweat, and cry for their country.

On the other hand, how did President Bill Clinton survive a crisis many people believed would bring down his presidency and send him off to a sunset of disgrace and humiliation? For sure, he had personality. When he told people, "I feel your pain," they believed him. But what really saved him from impeachment was smarts, intelligence well above the norm. He bamboozled some of America's best prosecutors and lawmakers by making his definition of "is" sound like a treatise for a new volume in the law school library. He led them to see accents in sentences they had not looked at closely before. He outsmarted them. Academic superiority saved his presidency. Where Winston Churchill led through personality, Bill Clinton led primarily through force.

"May the force be with you!" That sentence from the *Star Wars* movie a few years ago took on a life of its own among America's young people and movie fans. Slightly modified, those words found their way into the self-help world when a well-known guru from that arena spoke in our city on one occasion. The speaker spoke of God's Spirit as a force to increase sales and profits. "May his force be with you," he said as he closed his presentation.

Is the Holy Spirit just a force, or is the Spirit of God we profess belief in through this *Life Line* more than that? What does the source book say? A Bible study on the Holy Spirit reveals several personality characteristics that inanimate forces are incapable of possessing. It forces us to conclude that the Holy Spirit is a real person and not merely a force. More correctly, he is a person with force. He possesses power far beyond any other. Person always comes first with him, however, because who he is effects what he achieves.

PERSONALITY PLUS

What are some of these personality characteristics that the Bible notes about the Holy Spirit? Consider first his ability to reason. Paul writes about *"the mind of the Spirit" (Romans 8:27)*. Obviously, if the Spirit of God were purely impersonal energy or force, he would not be capable of thinking. Immediately following Paul's declaration about the Spirit's reasoning powers, the apostle adds that the Spirit also *"intercedes"* for us. He chooses the Greek word *entugchano*. It means to intervene, mediate, plead, or act on behalf of someone. Impersonal forces are also incapable of these things. It is a powerfully comforting and empowering idea Paul passes on to us. Elsewhere, he writes that Jesus is the *"one mediator between God and men" (1 Timothy 2:5)*. Now he lets us know that while the Son of God is our mediator in heaven, the Spirit of God is mediating for us on Earth.

Making and keeping peace in human relationships is probably the most difficult work any of us can ever do. I still tell every couple I marry that Sam Heslip defined a wedding service as an event where two sinners come together to combine their sins. I chuckle at that definition but I also point out that there is profound truth in Sam's humor. How do we make a relationship born in such an environment work? More than that, how can we make marriage fun, exciting, and fulfilling in the long term for both the bride and groom? Only by the Holy Spirit! He *"intercedes"* on our behalf.

In a broader sense, how do we achieve meaningful reconciliation where once there was devastating disagreement or where the biases of former generations have been passed on to children? The simple truth is we cannot. Only the Holy Spirit can! I am convinced that whether or not his presence is recognized, he is always at work when true and lasting peace is accomplished. No impersonal force can do it. The mark of victory over division in human relationships is not the absence of conflict but the presence of a reconciling spirit at work. In short, former enemies have to want to be friends. All sides must yearn for reconciliation. Where is that yearning born? It is born in our hearts by the Holy Spirit.

Other evidence that the Holy Spirit is personality is that he speaks. *"The Spirit said unto Philip..."* (Acts 8:29). Someone I know was scheduled to board a flight from one city to another. His trip to the airport seemed to be delayed by a string of unusual events. He arrived barely on time for his departure only by going faster than the speed limit and running some red lights, something he would normally not do. As he stood in line at the check-in desk, a compelling, even though inaudible, voice somewhere deep inside him told him very plainly not to take that flight. This man is not usually given to such experiences, but somehow he was so taken by this voice deep within that he dropped out of the line and made plans to catch a later flight. The flight he rushed to catch never reached its destination. It crashed into the ocean and everyone on board was killed. Where does such a still, small voice come from? Certainly not from an unspeaking, unfeeling force! It can only come from a person who knows the future and is looking out for us. He now believes that the voice within came from the same source as the voice that spoke to Elijah. *"There came a voice unto him,"* (1 Kings 19:13). This one who spoke to Moses in the burning bush now speaks to us through our burning hearts. He ignites our passions and causes us to act in ways that honor Christ. The real evidence that we believe in the Holy Spirit is found in our feet and hands and not just in feelings and words.

The Holy Spirit not only speaks and acts, he feels. He has emotion. No impersonal force can have feelings. For example, he loves: *"I beseech you, brethren, for the Lord Jesus Christ's sake, and for the love of the Spirit, that ye strive together with me in your prayers to God for me"* (Romans 15:30). He grieves, too. Paul cautions, *"Grieve not the holy Spirit of God, whereby ye are sealed unto the day of redemption"* (Ephesians 4:30). He also fellowships! Scripture encourages *"the communion of the Holy Ghost"* (2 Corinthians 13:14). The word for *"communion"* is *koinonia*, sometimes also translated as fellowship. All these emotional characteristics serve to remind us that when we say we believe in the Holy Spirit through this *Life Line* we are not talking about a thing but a real person.

THE IMPOSSIBILITY SPECIALIST

"The difficult we do immediately. The impossible takes a minute longer!" That humorous sign hangs in a print shop I sometimes visit. We all know that the impossible is that which can never happen. Yet, God specializes in accomplishing things once called impossible. *"The things which are impossible with men are possible with God" (Luke 18:27).* Such impossible tasks, it seems, are assigned to his Spirit. The Holy Spirit was the mission impossible agent in Christ's life. As we saw in chapter seven, he effected Christ's conception in the virgin Mary and told her about God's amazing plan for our redemption: *"The angel... said unto her, 'The Holy Ghost shall come upon thee, and the power of the Highest shall overshadow thee: therefore also that holy thing which shall be born of thee shall be called the Son of God'"* *(Luke 1:35).* Mary's world would have said it was impossible for a virgin to have a baby. Indeed, even in our world there are still some folks who say that. They need to meet this Holy Spirit. When Mary's betrothed, Joseph, was convinced that his beloved's condition was impossible without unfaithfulness on her part, he was told, *"Joseph, thou son of David, fear not to take unto thee Mary thy wife: for that which is conceived in her is of the Holy Ghost" (Matthew 1:20).* The same one who achieved Christ's conception was instrumental in his resurrection and, indeed, in ours. *"If the Spirit of him that raised up Jesus from the dead dwell in you, he that raised up Christ from the dead shall also quicken your mortal bodies by his Spirit that dwelleth in you" (Romans 8:11).*

RAISING CHAD

Think about it! This is a promise for you. The same Spirit that worked beyond all the horizons of human understanding to raise Christ from the dead now is promised to work in our lives. He brings us alive in ways we cannot design or imagine. He elevates us in mini reflections of the Lord's resurrection and takes us to new heights.

"I believe in the Holy Spirit." When we look across the years of our own lives, how can we not believe in him? In all our lives there is evidence of supernatural power at work to accomplish good things that have no human explanation. In a sense it can be said that our conception also is miraculous, though not, of course, on the same high level as our Lord's virgin birth. Think about a newborn baby. A special life force must go to work to turn two elements of what is otherwise messy human body matter into a beautiful human baby. It is no accident and no quirk of nature that we were conceived, regardless of the circumstances surrounding our origin. *"Thou sendest forth thy spirit, they are created" (Psalm 104:30).*

Chad, a good-looking high school junior, bemoaned the turmoil of his life. His litany of woe began with his girlfriend's recent rejection and his resultant poor grades. As we talked, he traced the story of his life of seventeen years. It sounded like a winding pathway through the garden of despair. Finally, his head hanging in a sense of unearned shame, Chad wept. "Now I've discovered that I should never have been born. This week I learned that my Mom and Dad were not married when I was conceived. I was just an accident!" I took Chad to the pages of the Bible and pointed out that, in God's world, there are no accidents. Every human being ever created is conceived first in God's mind and God always has a purpose for us. I reminded him of famous leaders and achievers conceived in circumstances like his. Sometimes we tend to forget that or ignore it. God has no unwanted children and there are no accidents of conception. That is why we must heed the Bible when it says, *"The Spirit itself beareth witness with our spirit, that we are the children of God" (Romans 8:16).*

As we talked further, Chad's sense of self-esteem and his hopes for the future were raised that day. Just as the Spirit raised up Jesus, he also raises us up when the circumstances around us seem too heavy to bear. *"And if (we are) children, then heirs; heirs of God, and joint-heirs with Christ; if so be that we suffer with him, that we may be also glorified together. For I reckon that the sufferings of this present time are not worthy to be compared with the glory which shall be revealed in us. For the earnest expectation of the creature waiteth for the manifestation of the sons of God. For the creature was made subject to vanity, not willingly, but by reason of him who hath subjected the same in hope, Because the creature itself also shall be delivered from the bondage of corruption into the glorious liberty of the children of God. For we know that the whole creation groaneth and travaileth in pain together until now. And not only they, but ourselves also, which have the firstfruits of the Spirit, even we ourselves groan within ourselves, waiting for the adoption, to wit, the redemption of our body. For we are saved by hope: but hope that is seen is not hope: for what a man seeth, why doth he yet hope for? But if we hope for that we see not, then do we with patience wait for it. Likewise the Spirit also helpeth our infirmities: for we know not what we should pray for as we ought: but the Spirit itself maketh intercession for us with groanings which cannot be uttered" (Romans 8:17-26).*

This Holy Spirit we believe in comes to us at God's ushering and lifts us above the circumstances of the now into the dream that is born for tomorrow through hope. Life is ultimately hopeless without him because the end of life without the Spirit is never good.

Like Chad, are there circumstances in the past and present that you would like to put into perspective? Are there issues you need to put behind you? Does shame sometimes play on your life's center court? Ask the Holy Spirit to lift you in his renewing power above whatever troubles you. Believe in him and he will. He is *"that Holy Spirit of promise, which is the earnest of our inheritance until the redemption of the purchased possession" (Ephesians 1:13,14)*. The Spirit guarantees, or seals, us for Christ.

This Holy Spirit, by his unique creative wonder, has brought us together through the words that are written on these pages. When we seek to know him, he orders these moments in our lives in such a way that we will come face-to-face with Jesus. That, finally, is his chief mission. He is the one who directs us to Christ.

Do you believe in this Holy Spirit? If you do, welcome him each day and invite him to move freely in your life. When you do, he will live his life out through you for Christ's sake.

Coming up is an introduction to the most amazing group of people anywhere on Earth. Read on and get connected.

CHAPTER SIXTEEN

What Is the One True Church?

What is it? It is at the same time local and universal. It is physical, yet spiritual. It lives in time, but is eternal. It is both visible and invisible. You could call it "God's wife." It is the most important organization in world history. What is it? It is the subject of this chapter. Read on! Find out! Get involved!

Ah, nostalgia! They say it just isn't what it used to be. "All the king's horses and all the king's men can't put the past together again!" Maybe that's just as well because I have a hunch that the good old days were once mourned as "these terrible times." There isn't much about yesteryear, that I can think of, that was better than what we know today. Yet, it doesn't hurt to reflect sometimes. It helps us see how far we have come and often makes us smile at what we had or how we did.

When you think about the past what comes to your mind first of all? A much beloved grandparent or parent now gone on? The Great Depression? The New Deal? The war? The old country? Your first day at school? Do you remember the hula-hoop? I do, but I could never get one to stay up. Maybe you could. Maybe thoughts of the past bring to your mind a picture from the old Sears catalog. Do you remember dancing the twist? How about the Charleston? Glass milk bottles sitting on your doorstep with the cream at the top? The Model T or the family outhouse? They all have their place in history. They were fun and practical in their time. Then, somehow they all passed on, replaced, at least for a while, by something new. Taken together, their passing symbolizes progress or, perhaps some folks would say, the fickleness of human nature. This *Life Line* is about something more permanent than all these things, an institution that preceded them all and continues to flourish today all around the world.

139

THE MOST IMPORTANT ORGANIZATION IN WORLD HISTORY

"I believe in the holy catholic church and the communion of the saints." *"Christ loved the church, and gave himself for it" (Ephesians 5:25).* The church for which Jesus died on the cross is the most important organization in the history of the world. When I say that, I mean it to be thought of in a number of ways. It is the most important, first of all, because the Son of God gave his life for it. No other society has been given that much love!

Second, the church is the most important of all institutions because no other has touched as many lives in as many nations. It is also the most important because of its significance in human history. Wherever the church has gone throughout the world, hospitals, institutions of learning, and great worship centers have been established to encourage people in Christ's name. Having said all this, the *Life Line* about believing in the holy catholic church is one of the most controversial in the Creed. Some folks are hesitant to make this declaration. From my position in front of our congregation, I have observed, on occasion, that some folks cease to speak just before this line and resume their profession when we say the line following it. So, let's think about what this fascinating *Life Line* says.

MARCHING TO GLORY!

The first declaration the Creed authors make about the church is that it is "holy." They called it "the holy catholic church." *"Israel was holiness unto the LORD" (Jeremiah 2:3).* What does this mean?

First, it might be good to state clearly what it does not mean. Holy does not mean perfect. Holy and perfect are not synonyms.

In the Old Testament, holiness carries two ideas with it. They are separation and purity. Israel was holy in that it was unlike the nations around it. For one thing, there was a commitment to monotheism. Israel had one God. The other nations were polytheistic. They had many gods. As we have seen in previous chapters, this was the primary offense that Elijah addressed on Mount Carmel when he threw down, as it were, his gauntlet in the face of the Baal prophets. *"If the LORD be God, follow him: but if Baal, then follow him" (1 Kings 18:21).* Following Israel's one God, Jehovah, called for a second kind of separation. Jehovah called Israel to a lifestyle that was distinct from the polytheistic pagan nations around them. Theirs was a journey toward purity, or goodness.

The New Testament enlarges this idea of demonstrated holiness. *"Be ye holy; for I am holy" (1 Peter 1:16).* This is a restatement of an Old Testament principle, except that now the charge is not just for holiness before a few neighboring nations, but for holy living to be exhibited before the entire world. Holiness like this calls us to be totally devoted and dedicated to God and his principles. That means we are committed to showing goodness by how we live.

Once again, the call to holiness is not a call to sinless perfection. The New Testament church was no more perfect than its Old Testament counterpart. Just as David the adulterer and murderous schemer and Moses the killer and Abraham the liar and fornicator were part of the church in the Old Testament, Paul, the self-professed chief sinner, was part of the New Testament church. The call to be holy is not a call to be perfect in either case; yet, it is very definitely a call in that direction. Holy means being sorry for our sins and repenting from them, that is, working to be better in the strength of the Holy Spirit. Paul illustrates this better than anyone else with a word of personal testimony: *"Not as though I had already attained, either were already perfect: but I follow after, if that I may apprehend that for which also I am apprehended of Christ Jesus. Brethren, I count not myself to have apprehended: but this one thing I do, forgetting those things which are behind, and reaching forth unto those things which are before, I press toward the mark for the prize of the high calling of God in Christ Jesus"* (Philippians 3:12-14). Paul acknowledges his continuing imperfection but he also states his determination to press forward in pursuit of his calling. His is no casual commitment. He *"presses"* toward perfection. The Greek for press is *dioko,* meaning the kind of hard discipline a winning athlete endures in preparation for a major event. He is marching toward the glory of perfection; not there yet, but he keeps on marching. And, so do we!

We are still a long way from holiness in the church at the beginning of the new millennium. We have coined attractive sounding words that often seem to be designed to enable us to accommodate some behavior that goes on in the world around us. Words like pluralism have birthed heresies that make our lines of separation fuzzy sometimes. They often make it difficult to discern between the church and our culture. Not only that, but society has found clever ways to accommodate certain churchy words in its everyday language. A young woman who was once the focus of a very public scandal with a prominent married man was being interviewed by Barbara Walters on an ABC News television program. What had she learned from her promiscuous relationship and its aftermath, Barbara Walters asked her. She promptly replied, "I've learned that before I get involved with another married man, I have to pray about it." We might wonder what she meant by prayer or what she thought there could be to pray about in a situation like that. Yet, comments like that come from the other side of the church/culture fence because we have not always sent out a clear statement of our distinctive differences.

The word *church* is itself an illustrator of what being holy means. It comes from the Greek word *ekklesia.* Like some of the other Greek words we have considered in this book, *ekklesia* comes from combining two other Greek words. In this case, the first part of the word is *ek.* It means to be out, or away, from something; thus, separation is implied. We get our English word *exit* and the prefix *ex* from it. The last part of the word *ekklesia* is *klesia.* Like one of the words we considered in the last chapter, *klesia* comes from *kaleo,* or call. The Greek word for church means people called to be different, or called out ones. To believe in this "holy" church means to be distinct from society.

The second part of the *Life Line* sometimes evokes a certain level of controversy among Christians. A member of a congregation where I was speaking declared, "I never say that line." "May I ask why?" I asked him. He responded, "Because I'm not a Roman Catholic." Right away, I could see the issue for him. It is the same reason why others who are Presbyterians, Lutherans, Methodists, and Episcopalians, to name but a few, sometimes hesitate to make this affirmation. You will note, however, that the Roman Catholic Church is not mentioned here, or elsewhere, among the words of the Apostles' Creed.

The catholicity affirmed in the Creed is altogether different from that. This catholic is pre-Reformation in context. The church we profess belief in is catholic but not Roman. Catholic comes from two Greek words: *kata,* meaning throughout, and *holos,* meaning the whole. Catholic, in its essence, means broad in scope or universal in the sense that it reaches across the world. "The holy catholic church" is the church that raises Christ's banner faithfully on every continent. It has been my privilege to see this church in action from Belfast to Bangkok; from Hong Kong to Hollywood; from Nashville to Nairobi; and places in between. It is a great church because its Master made a great promise: *"I will build my church; and the gates of hell shall not prevail against it"* (Matthew 16:18).

THE INDESTRUCTIBLE ARMY

Rome never raised a viler emperor than Diocletian. He was born in the middle of the third century after Christ. As talented and energetic as he was, he lost his life to hatred. He determined to eradicate Christ's Church from the face of the earth. He was so committed to his plan and so certain of its success, that he erected a huge stone column as a monument to himself. Inscribed on it were these words: "HE EXTERMINATED THE CHRISTIANS FROM EARTH." Can you imagine the embarrassment Diocletian might feel if he were to see his monument today? Another Roman leader, Constantine, ordered a huge coffin built to symbolize his intention "to bury the Galilean and his people once and for all." He soon learned that Christ will occupy no tomb nor will his church be placed in any coffin. In time, realizing the error of his ways, Constantine became a Christian. Unable to destroy the church Jesus started, he joined it!

The symbol of the Waldensian Christians features a blacksmith's anvil surrounded by worn-out hammers. Underneath are these words: "One anvil. Many hammers." People who beat up on the church wear out but, like the anvil, the church stands firm. This living organism called the church of the Lord Jesus Christ cannot be destroyed. It is an indestructible army. Today it is more catholic, or universally far reaching, than ever before.

"Verily, verily, I say unto you, He that believeth on me, the works that I do shall he do also; and greater works than these shall he do; because I go unto my Father" (John 14:12). Catholic, as the Creed authors understood it, is what Jesus meant when he spoke these words. He was not saying they would outperform his miracles: Saving the lost, raising the dead, feeding more than five thousand from a little boy's lunch are pretty much unbeatable feats. What could anyone do to surpass them? They are as miraculous as one can get. Instead, Jesus is saying that his church would take his light and shine it in every land. If you believe that, you believe in "the holy catholic church."

THE GREAT GO MISSION

To profess "catholic" as the Creed intends, is to profess our personal commitment to missions. One cannot say, "I believe in the holy catholic church" and not get involved in world evangelization. When Jesus left the disciples with his Great Commission, *"Go ye therefore, and teach all nations, baptizing them in the name of the Father, and of the Son, and of the Holy Ghost: Teaching them to observe all things whatsoever I have commanded you: and, lo, I am with you alway, even unto the end of the world" (Matthew 28:19,20),* he was reaffirming the missionary heart of the Father. In the Old Testament we see this first in the promise made to Abram: *"In thee shall all families of the earth be blessed" (Genesis 12:3).* This passage, like the one just cited, tells us that God is a missionary God. Therefore his church is a missionary fellowship.

A wonderful legend recounts Christ's return to heaven. The angel Gabriel saw him and said, "Master, you suffered terribly for the people down there." The Lord agreed. Gabriel continued, "Do they now all know and appreciate how great your love is?" Jesus replied, "No. Not yet. Right now only a handful of people around Jerusalem know." Gabriel, perplexed for lack of understanding, asked, "What have you done to get your story out?" Jesus replied, "I asked Peter, James, John, and a few more of my friends to go and tell it. Once they tell others, the others will, in turn, also tell others. Eventually, my story will go all over the world. Everybody will know who I am and how much I gave to save them." Gabriel frowned, skeptically. "But what if they grow weary? What if they forget? What if they just stop telling? Haven't you any backup plan?" Jesus replied, "No. I have no backup plan. I'm really counting on them."

There is still no backup plan! Christ is counting on you and me to tell his story. In this *Life Line*, we assure all who are listening (and God is surely in that audience!) that we will carry out his missionary mandate. We will go wherever he calls us. That is what we mean when, through this line in the Creed, we call ourselves "catholic" Christians.

THE INVISIBLE CHURCH

The church is not only universal, however. It is eternal. It exists on Earth and in heaven: *"Every creature which is in heaven...heard I saying, Blessing, and honour, and glory, and power, be unto him that sitteth upon the throne, and unto the Lamb for ever and ever"(Revelation 5:13).*

John Calvin called this the invisible church. For him, the church consists of two parts. One is visible. Everybody can see it as it gathers to worship on Earth. The other is invisible because earthlings know it only through the eyes of faith. Its members are all the faithful from the beginning of time. Through his church all around the world, God is calling out people to live with him for all eternity.

The church of this *Life Line* is catholic. Its impact is universal and eternal. It is all over the world and will not be stopped. The church is also local. This local version of the church is "the communion of the saints."

SAINTS ALIVE!

"How is your husband?" a woman asked her friend whom she had not seen in a while. "Oh," replied the friend, "he is a real saint." The first retorted, "Oh, dear, aren't you lucky? Mine is still alive!"

Are you like that enquiring woman? Do you think saints are dead people especially elevated above ordinary folks like you and me? When you think of saints, does your mind conjure up a picture of a stained glass window you've seen in a church somewhere? I have good news for you! St. Paul begins his letter to the Church in Ephesus, *"Paul, an apostle of Jesus Christ by the will of God, to the saints which are at Ephesus" (Ephesians 1:1).* Did you see it? *"Saints,"* he calls them! Just before that, he wrote to the Corinthians, *"All the saints salute you" (2 Corinthians 13:13).* These don't sound like greetings to or from dead people, do they? That is because they are very much alive. The Old Testament Hebrew word most often translated *saint* is *kadhosh*. The New Testament word for *saint* is *hagioi*. A study of these two words reveals two very interesting facts. One is that they are applied with practical uniformity to groups, not individuals. The second thing we learn from studying the Bible on this issue is that all the saints are alive. They live both on Earth and in heaven. There is not a single dead saint anywhere in the entire Bible.

How does someone become a saint? Well, we've just seen that you can't die to be one. So, if you want to be a saint, the first thing you need to do is to find a way to keep on living for all eternity. The only way to do that is to trust Jesus. He says, *"Whosoever liveth and believeth in me shall never die" (John 11:26).*

There is a second Bible requirement for sainthood. What do you think it is? Did you say "sinless living?" No, for that is impossible as long as we are in this world. The Bible says, *"If we say that we have no sin, we deceive ourselves, and the truth is not in us" (1 John 1:8).* Even worse than that indictment is the one that follows: *"If we say that we have not sinned, we make him a liar" (1 John 1:10).* In other words, to say that we no longer are sinners is to make God a sinner! Can you think of a worse sin than that? I can't!

So, what is this second requirement for living sainthood? Very simply, it is to keep on following Jesus. Just keep on! When life is hard and you feel like throwing in the towel on your faith, don't dare do it. Just keep on following. This is the second Bible requirement for being a saint. Call it consistent Christian living. So, when we say we believe in "the communion of the saints," we are talking about local congregations and church groups on Earth where Christ's gospel is faithfully preached and the word of God is lived out.

SINNERS EMERITUS WE ARE NOT!

Are you actively involved in a local congregation? I hope you are. The Bible instructs all Christians to be with other Christians. *"Let us hold fast the profession of our faith without wavering; (for he is faithful that promised;) And let us consider one another to provoke unto love and to good works: Not forsaking the assembling of ourselves together, as the manner of some is; but exhorting one another: and so much the more, as ye see the day approaching" (Hebrews 10:23-25).*

I'm a pastor. I speak in various places and travel and write some. Yet, my first love is being pastor of a local congregation. In my position, I have seen the church from the inside and I confess that everything I have witnessed has not pleased me. Churches and local congregations do things that none of us can be proud about. The reason for that is very simple: Local churches are not havens for perfect saints. They are hospitals for pitiful sinners. Every church I know—especially mine—is pastored by a sinner. Some things that happen in congregations hurt people. That saddens me greatly. Yet, it happens because sinners are going to do things that hurt other people. Or, dare I say, "Sinners will hurt other sinners"? I also know that preachers and local church pastors make mistakes. I know this one does, for sure. Sometimes we make really big mistakes and people are hurt as a result of what we do. None of us, I hope, mean to do that. Still, we do. And sometimes people get hurt enough, angry enough, or turned off enough to quit the church. The writer to the Hebrews says, "Don't do that!" *"Let us consider one another to provoke unto love and to good works: Not forsaking the assembling of ourselves together."* If you have been hurt by someone in your church and have stopped participating in the life of God's people, please allow me to offer my condolences and encourage you to get back to church and try again. I understand what it is to be hurt by the church. Every pastor I know has been hurt by a church at some time or other. Yet, we know we dare not forsake this organization established, commissioned, and abundantly blessed by Jesus Christ. When all is said and done, it is a privilege to be part of the only institution the Bible says God started through his Son.

That people get hurt in churches should not surprise us too much. After all, it was the religious leaders who led the charge against Jesus when he walked among us to start his church. His best friends deserted and disowned him when he most needed their help. In spite of that, he came back to the church right after his resurrection. The first thing he did after he rose from the dead was to look up the very people who abandoned him. Why would he do that? Because Jesus Christ is not a quitter! He will never give up on his church. Make him, and not the people who may have hurt you, your example. Show Jesus you really do believe in his "holy catholic church and the communion of the saints." Then, read on. In the next chapter, I'm going to tell you the best way to get back at people who hurt you.

"The Spirit and the bride say, Come. And let him that heareth say, Come. And let him that is athirst come. And whosoever will, let him take the water of life freely" (Revelation 22:17).

The church is the bride of Christ. This is an image that is repeated a number of times in Scripture. As the bride, or wife, of Jesus, our mission is foundationally threefold. We are empowered to help make this bride ready for her big day: *"Blessed are they which are called unto the marriage supper of the Lamb"* (Revelation 19:9). That is us! Our mission on Earth is to exalt her Lord in worship, equip his laity for work, and evangelize the lost through witness. Let us demonstrate our belief by resolving now to do these things better than ever before.

CHAPTER SEVENTEEN

When Someone Hurts Me, What's the Best Revenge?

"I don't get mad. I get even!" he screamed. Is "getting even" a good idea when someone takes advantage of you? What is the most effective way to deal with people who hurt you? We've all experienced it: Someone trusted betrayed us. Someone to whom we gave our heart did us dirty. Do we strike back when that happens? Fight fire with fire? Do we look for revenge? Do we retaliate? In this chapter, we'll learn the best thing to do when someone sins against us. We'll find out about our deepest need and God's biggest idea. Read on.

"Love your enemies. It drives them nuts!" When France's King Louis XII was preparing to ascend to the throne, his enemies conspired to kidnap and imprison him. They determined to do anything short of taking his life to prevent his official coronation. Their best efforts to accomplish this goal failed. The crown was placed on Louis XII's head at a ceremony in the palace. Immediately afterward, his counselors recommended to King Louis XII that he seek revenge. As France's unquestioned king, he could order the army to ferret out his enemies and bring them one-by-one to the guillotine. A list of rogues was composed. Names and titles of every known conspirator were listed on it. The completed

147

list was delivered to the King in his throne room. Counselors and supporters watched and waited silently as Louis XII surveyed the names before him. They expected King Louis to issue a royal decree that would bring his enemies to a speedy death. Louis hesitated then asked a scribe to bring him a jar of red ink. He took the quill from the inkpot and placed a red cross beside every single name. "Go forth," he declared, "and tell them all that the cross beside their name is not the mark of revenge but a pledge to forgive in the name of the crucified Savior, who said we must forgive our enemies." He paused, and then passed the list to his chief advisor saying, "Tell them all that, in the name of Christ, King Louis XII of France forgives you."

GOD'S BIGGEST IDEA

"I believe in the forgiveness of sins." Every other *Life Line* we have looked at so far hangs on this one. It is the most amazingly beautiful life principle any sinner can ever hear and the biggest idea God ever had. Think about it: God the Father Almighty, Maker of heaven and earth, so loved the world that he gave Jesus Christ, his only Son, our Lord, who was conceived by the Holy Spirit, born of the Virgin Mary, suffered under Pontius Pilate, was crucified, dead, buried, and descended into hell. On the third day, he rose from the dead and ascended into heaven. God, through Christ, gave his Holy Spirit for his church so that we might tell every sinner in the world the truth that Isaiah the prophet saw seven hundred years before Jesus Christ was born: *"The LORD hath laid on him the iniquity of us all" (Isaiah 53:6)*. Jesus confirmed it: *"God so loved the world, that he gave his only begotten Son, that whosoever believeth in him should not perish,.but have everlasting life. For God sent not his Son into the world to condemn the world; but that the world through him might be saved" (John 3:16,17)*. John, the disciple Jesus loved, restated it: *"If we confess our sins, he is faithful and just to forgive us our sins, and to cleanse us from all unrighteousness" (1 John 1:9)*. Is this not the most universally needed and amazingly beautiful truth your heart has ever heard?

THE FELLOWSHIP OF THE FORGIVEN

The forgiveness of sins is the essence of the Christian gospel. *"Thus it is written, and thus it behoved Christ to suffer, and to rise from the dead the third day: And that repentance and remission of sins should be preached in his name among all nations" (Luke 24:46,47)*.

Our church edifice sits squarely at the heart of Pittsburgh's Golden Triangle. There is probably no more centrally located building in the entire downtown area. Within a block or two are housed the headquar-

148

ters or major offices of more than a dozen corporations whose names are household words all across the land. Not far away are the city and county offices. Into this locale, more than 130,000 people flood five days each week to work. They are joined by at least that many more who come downtown daily to take care of business. Our mission is to reach these people with the gospel of Jesus Christ. Every day folk step inside our building to pray, seek spiritual guidance, or ask for material help. Each day they pass the sign that says,

> *Friend, enter in...*
> *This hallowed place;*
> *Has been a rendezvous of grace.*
> *Time and again a weary soul*
> *Has come in sore and gone out whole.*
> *Friend, enter in.*

It is our ambition to create an environment where the spiritual needs of every person entering are met in Christ's name. To fulfill every opportunity we present the claims of Christ, either through written publications or verbally.

THE BEST PLACE FOR HYPOCRITES

Just last week, a young man came in seeking financial aid. He showed up just before one of our midweek worship services and I invited him to worship with us. He declined, saying, "I believe in God, but I don't believe in the church." It was a strange statement for someone who came to the church requesting assistance. "May I ask why?" I inquired in response. "Because," he protested, "the church is full of hypocrites!" "I know," I assured him. Then I added, "If you can think of a better place for them, tell me where it is and I'll take this group to it!" He was stumped. He came to worship. I claimed for him God's promise: *"My word...shall not return unto me void, but it shall accomplish that which I please, and it shall prosper in the thing whereto I sent it" (Isaiah 55:11).*

The church is not a country club for people who have reached some ecstatic state of sinless perfection. It is the fellowship of forgiven sinners. The church is not a society for people who no longer do wrong things. It is God's safe-house for people like me who sin grievously against God and keep coming back because they need another dose of pardoning grace. That is why Christ committed his message of forgiveness to the church.

THE ETERNAL EQUALIZERS

There are only two great equalizers that unite the pompous and the paupers of our world. Two unchanging realities join together people

149

from every background and ethnicity. The first is that the greatest need we each have is for forgiveness. The second is that because of God's grace all our sins were accounted against Christ on his cross at Calvary. Through him alone we find forgiveness.

> *My sin—O, the bliss of this glorious thought!*
> *My sin, not in part, but the whole,*
> *Is nailed to the cross and I bear it no more;*
> *Praise the Lord, praise the Lord, O my soul!* [28]

Horatio Spafford praised God that his sin "not in part, but the whole" was nailed to Christ's cross. How much of your sin was on the cross? The Bible says all of it was. He cleanses us *"from all unrighteousness" (1 John 1:9).* There is, therefore, no room for guilt or shame—among the most crippling of human emotions—in a Christian's life. Forgiveness is our deepest need and God's highest achievement.

A father and his son became verbally entangled in a family argument. Strong words were spoken hastily and loudly by each of them. As a result, the lad stormed out of the family home in a rage. The night came and he did not return home. The night gave way to the new day and there was an empty place at the family breakfast table. That place remained glaringly vacant for several days. Out of his own growing desperation and in response to the pleas of the fear-terrorized wife and mother of his son, the father began to search for his boy. Night upon night he tromped the city streets, searching all his son's old haunts. He did not find him there. He visited the lad's friends but they all said they did not know his whereabouts. Finally, that father, now greatly concerned about his son's well being, placed an advertisement in the personals column of the local newspaper. It read simply, "Sandy, all is forgiven. Meet me in front of the City Hall this Saturday at noon. Your mother and I still love you. Dad." On Saturday at noon, fifty young men called Sandy gathered in front of the City Hall. Each of them came hoping that his father was the one who would be waiting there. Forty-nine left disappointed.

Since Calvary's cross, Jesus Christ, by his Holy Spirit, has been advertising his forgiveness, calling your name and mine, and saying, "Meet me at the cross. All is forgiven. The Father and I still love you." If something from the past troubles your soul, you will find his forgiveness by going to the cross. God transformed that one great heinous act of injustice into the most amazing act of reunion and forgiving mercy that the world will ever know.

"The LORD hath laid on him the iniquity of us all" (Isaiah 53:6). Isaiah's declaration contains universality that many Christians fail to see. He forgives *"us all."* It means that God forgives every sin by every sinner

through the cross of Jesus. It is not just the people we read about in the Bible who are forgiven. Christ's forgiving grace is not restricted to Noah for drunken shamelessness; nor Abraham for lies and fornication with Hagar; nor Moses the short-fused murderer; nor Miriam the gossip; nor Thomas the doubter; nor quick-tempered Peter; nor self-righteous John; nor even the penitent thief hanging beside Jesus on the cross. It is for all of us who are guilty of these or any other sins. It is for the world. How does a Moslem or Hindu or Buddhist or Jew or Rastafarian find forgiveness? Only through Jesus! *"God laid on Jesus the iniquity of us all."* That is why we must tell this news urgently to the entire world. There is no forgiveness outside Christ.

FORGIVING EACH OTHER

"Forgive us our debts, as we forgive our debtors"... "If ye forgive men their trespasses, your heavenly Father will also forgive you: But if ye forgive not men their trespasses, neither will your Father forgive your trespasses" *(Matthew 6:14,15).* The only repeated statement Jesus makes in the Sermon on the Mount is about our need to be forgiven and to forgive each other. What amazing power Christ entrusts to us in the Lord's Prayer! For an instant, we at the same time control forgiveness both on Earth and in heaven. He teaches us to ask for forgiveness to the extent that we each are willing to forgive.

When an Irish Republican Army bomb killed Gordon Wilson's daughter, several options were his. One was the typical tit-for-tat revenge that has kept Northern Ireland's terrorist groups in the killing business for years. Gordon Wilson, however, chose a better way. He stifled a backlash by opposing paramilitary groups with a Christian common sense declaration: "It is enough! I have lost my daughter. What is to be gained if another parent loses another child? I choose to bear no ill will and harbor no grudge." Attempting to turn rancor into reconciliation, Gordon Wilson went so far as to meet with leaders of the group that slaughtered his daughter and expressed his forgiveness face-to-face. His example of living out the message of turning the other cheek showed whom the real soldier was. It told the world who really loved Ireland. Gordon Wilson demonstrated strength that requires super-human effort. As that was true for him, it is also true for us. It is not natural for us to forgive when we have suffered.

HOW FORGIVENESS WORKS

How does this forgiveness work? First, we start by accepting the forgiveness Jesus Christ offers us for all our sins. We must hold nothing of our evil thoughts and wrong ways back from him. Second, we realize that not only does he forgive, he chooses not to remember. *"I, even I, am he that blotteth out thy transgressions for mine own sake, and will not remember thy sins" (Isaiah 43:25).* Third, we ask ourselves what kind of forgiveness we want. Surely the answer is that we want absolute forgiveness with nothing held to our account. Having done this, we now make ourselves available to be channels of forgiving grace toward others, applying Christ's Golden Rule: *"All things whatsoever ye would that men should do to you, do ye even so to them" (Matthew 7:12).* It is always easier to forgive when we realize how much we have been forgiven.

Forgiveness like this means we forego thoughts of striking back. We refuse to repay gossip with gossip or a bad deed with a worse one. It calls us to replace feelings of resentment and anger with good will. It means we seek the offender's best interests in all things rather than wishing him or her harm. It calls us to initiate concrete steps to restore good relationships.

Not only do we forgive, we choose not to remember. We have no power to erase what we remember, but we can choose which parts of them will receive our primary attention. We can change agonizing past memories into future hopes.

How do we do it? First, by focusing on the good parts of our bad past. A couple who lost their son in an automobile accident said, "We give thanks for the twenty years of joy he brought us. He blessed us in ways we would never have known without him." They chose to remember the happy times over the terrible night they received the call from the hospital emergency room asking them to come quickly. Second, by remembering honestly. A drunk driver killed him, but their son was speeding at the time. They said, "His high rate of speed made the impact worse. It contributed to the severity of his injuries." Third, by remembering with reality. The fact is that pain is inherent to close human relationships. From the moment we invest in a special relationship and give our love away, there is almost always a guarantee that one day tears will flow. Hurts, death, or other separation will cause one of us to cry. When we consider the tradeoff, however, we would be willing to do it again. An old saying goes, "Better to have loved and lost than never to have loved at all!"

IT WAS THE BEST OF TIMES
IT WAS THE WORST OF RELATIONSHIPS

"Be ye kind one to another, tenderhearted, forgiving one another, even as God for Christ's sake hath forgiven you" (Ephesians 4:32). What if I don't want to forgive? There is a great danger in withholding forgiveness and

saying the Lord's Prayer. It is that we ask God for a shorter measure of grace for others than we need for ourselves. When we say the line *"Forgive us our debts, as we forgive our debtors" (Matthew 6:12)*, we are praying, "Give me as much forgiveness as I give." In effect, we short-change ourselves where we most need grace. Because we are forgiven in Christ, we are called to be forgiving people. Not only is there no room in the Christian life for shame and guilt, there is no room for animosity. Life is too brief and too uncertain to do otherwise.

For a time, at least so far as Charles Dickens was concerned, there was no more misnamed man in England than William Makepeace Thackeray. It might be said that Dickens could not make peace with Thackeray and that Thackeray had a dickens of a time with Dickens. The two were the leading literary geniuses of the English-speaking world in their time. Yet, because they each possessed a fiercely competitive spirit and a strong ego, they could not stand one another. Neither had a kind word for the other. To make matters worse, Thackeray, the author of *Vanity Fair,* used his position as a writer for the weekly magazine *Punch* to ridicule Dickens and his work. Dickens publicly returned the volley at every opportunity. He constantly criticized Thackeray as a person and a writer. Their animosity grew. Just before Christmas 1863 they encountered each other on a London street. Each ignored the presence of the other and they passed without speaking. Thackeray had second thoughts. He turned back and extended his hand in friendship to Dickens. Dickens, poker-faced, refused to take it. That evening as he said his prayers, Dickens came under conviction that he, a disciple of the forgiving Christ, should have seized that moment to demonstrate his Master's pardon. He should have initiated forgiveness instead of withholding it. Moreover, he should have done so with warmth and grace. Even though it was late in the evening, Dickens arose and went out to offer Thackeray true reconciliation. As he traveled toward Thackeray's home, his old animosity gave way to grace. He realized that there was enough room in the world of English literature for the two of them and that they could compliment each other rather than be enemies. That evening the two great writers reconciled. They vowed to put their old animosities behind them. Soon after that Thackeray died suddenly. Dickens stood among the chief mourners at the graveside of his friend grateful that the two had reconciled before it was forever too late.

"I believe in the forgiveness of sins" is a *Life Line* with both vertical and horizontal dimensions. If we belong to Jesus, we are to receive the forgiveness he offers and initiate forgiveness in his name. *"Let not the sun go down upon your wrath" (Ephesians 4:26)*. This *Life Line* professing belief in forgiveness has an earthly and a heavenly dimension to it.

THE MYTH OF SELF-FORGIVENESS

"Every Sunday I say that I believe in the forgiveness of sins and yet I can't forgive myself. Please help me." Jayne was troubled by memories of an immoral relationship from many years before. It haunted her constantly. Secular psychologists have promoted the idea of self-forgiveness. Yet, the Bible never speaks about such a phenomenon. Scripture says only that we need God's forgiveness and that we are commanded to extend forgiveness to one another in Christ's name. It never speaks of a need to forgive ourselves. What could I say to Jayne in response to her plea for help?

Usually, when someone struggles with the idea of needing self-forgiveness, they have bought into this false pop-psychology notion. Almost always this grows out of a failure to comprehend and apply God's grace to a particular sin in their life. Jayne could not believe that God would forgive a sin like hers. The answer to her dilemma lay in these words: *"If we confess our sins, he is faithful and just to forgive us our sins, and to cleanse us from all unrighteousness"* *(1 John 1:9)*. The word *confess* means to agree with God that our sin was against him more than any other. *"Against thee, thee only, have I sinned, and done this evil in thy sight" (Psalm 51:4)*. When we agree with God that we have sinned against him, the Bible makes us a double-barreled offer of forgiveness.

Three key words speak of God's action in 1 John 1:9. The first is *faithful*. The Greek word means *consistent, trustworthy, dependable, reliable*. It says that God always, without exception, forgives our confession. Jesus says, *"Him that cometh to me I will in no wise cast out" (John 6:37)*. He is *faithful*. He forgives every confessed sin. The second key word is *just*. It speaks of God's justice. God is *"just, and the justifier of him which believeth in Jesus" (Romans 3:26)*. When the Greek text says he is *just,* it uses a word that speaks about God's impartiality, foundational honesty, and fairness. That is, he not only forgives every confessed sin, he forgives every confessing Christian. There is a third key word, also. It is the word translated *"all."* The word means *thoroughness, completeness, entirety*. When we come in confession to God, he cleans us up completely.

When we feel like Jayne, there are, finally, only two possible reasons. The first is that we will not accept God's promise and apply it to our own lives. The second reason is that we have subconsciously set a standard for forgiveness that is higher than God's standards. That is demagoguery, the establishment of a new god whom we have, at least for the moment, set above the Lord God. It is to effectively proclaim that Jesus' cross was not enough.

THE VICTORY CALL

But, the cross was enough! For that reason, we must believe and practice our belief in the forgiveness of sins. The final word from Christ's cross was *"teleo,"* translated *"It is finished" (John 19:30).* Before the cross, a complicated system of sacrifices was used to atone for sin. It was never sufficient and the sacrifice of atonement had to be performed often. Jesus became the final sacrifice. *"It is finished"* means to have paid a debt in full. He went to the cross to finish God's salvation work on our behalf. He paid a debt he did not owe because we owed a debt we could not pay. He who was sinless took our sin upon himself and bought us the victory. When he died, there was nothing more to pay, nor will there be ever again.

Joseph Conrad had just finished writing a lengthy and intense novel about domination and rescue. Because Conrad's native language was Polish, the task of working out precise English words and phrases was often quite difficult for him. When he finally completed the book, he scrawled a single word across the last page. It was not the word "finished" or "completed," but the word "Victory!" That word became the title of his novel.

On the cross, before committing his spirit into the Father's hands, Jesus, too, said, *"It is finished!"* That is our victory cry. All was completed in the atonement plan of God. He won our victory and that is why we must believe in the forgiveness of sin.

In the next chapter, we will explore answers to the most universally asked question in human history. Read on and hear about a better than lifetime guarantee.

CHAPTER EIGHTEEN

Is There Life After Death?

The oldest book in the Bible asks a question that the smartest people in the information age still ponder: "If a man die, shall he live again?" (Job 14:14). What do you think? Is there life after death? What happens when we die? Where are our loved ones who are dead? What does the Bible say? Read on and find the answer to the most commonly asked question in the world.

It was more by accident than design that the brilliant Christopher Wren is remembered primarily as England's greatest architect. The multi-talented son of the chaplain to King Charles I of England could have made his name and fortune in any number of fields. He was a professor of astronomy at Oxford University before his thirtieth birthday. He was also a mathematical scholar with few equals in his time. Architecture, in fact, was at first only a hobby for him. He liked to draw. He enjoyed designing things. In time, his avocation became his profession. At the age of 29, Christopher Wren was appointed to the prestigious position of Surveyor General to the Royal Court.

Saint Paul's Cathedral was consecrated as a place of worship more than one thousand years before Christopher Wren was born. When London's Great Fire destroyed the old church in 1666, Wren was commissioned to design a new church that would in all ways surpass Saint Paul's pre-fire splendor. He worked for seven years drawing up his plans. His design, based on a Latin cross, incorporated much of the stonework left from the former building. At its transept, a large dome would be the heart of the finished structure. It would pull the whole design together. Christopher Wren and his building superintendent stood with the chief stonemason

157

for the new cathedral. The three men considered the kind of keystone they might use to mark the building's heart. They dispatched an illiterate laborer to find a stone of approximately the shape and size they needed. Searching through the rubble of the former building, the laborer uncovered a fragment of a stone that the fire's heat had split into two pieces. He brought it to the three men. The size was good but the shape left something to be desired. Finally, someone decided to turn the stone over. When the stone was reversed, they found a Latin word inscribed upon it. That word was *RESURGAM*. It means *"I'll rise again!"* What better name for the stone that would be central to the new St. Paul's Cathedral.

OUR RESURGAM

"I believe in the resurrection of the body and the life everlasting." *"Now is Christ risen from the dead, and become the firstfruits of them that slept" (1 Corinthians 15:20).* Earlier we looked at the *Life Line* that affirms Christ's resurrection. Because Jesus defeated death, *Resurgam* is carved into the life of every Christian. Our Lord declares, *"Because I live, ye shall live also" (John 14:19).*

In the challenges and chances of life that befall us in this world, by holding to these stout *Life Lines* and the Bible promises upon which each of them is based, we are able to rise above the suffering, sorrow, and calamity that lies all around us. Let's be honest. There are times when life makes no sense. Probably no one knows this better than a pastor. Being called upon to minister in the face of senseless tragedies and seemingly pointless suffering is foundational to what we do. Sometimes our best human attempts to make the pieces of life's jigsaw puzzle fit together sound silly and simplistic. The only thing that helps us move through tragedies and the big questions that often surround them is that all the answers are not in yet for us. *"For we know in part, and we prophesy in part" (1 Corinthians 13:9).* It is the Bible's promise that we shall go where the resurrected Jesus is and find answers to all our unrequited questions, giving us hope in the face of this world's senselessness.

THE BIG EVENT

In John Irving's thought-provoking novel *A Prayer for Owen Meany,* Irving's key character has some profound words that indicate he understands the faith spelled out in the *Life Lines* of this Creed. Owen says, "Easter is the main event; if you don't believe the resurrection, you're not a Christian."

Owen Meany is right! Easter is the main event for Christians. Without the resurrection of Jesus, we have no more hope than a jungle wood-worshipper. Without his resurrection and its principle implication for our lives, Christianity fits in the same file folder as all the other religious systems in the world. In Jesus' resurrection and its subsequent assurance that we too shall rise from the dead, we have the only message of hope there is in our world. All other religious systems are about keeping laws and dead ends. Christianity is different because it is about a Leader who died and is alive again, and willing to come and live in our hearts if we invite him. What is more, he will stay with us all through this life, leading us through a series of mini-resurrections in the face of day-to-day senselessness until he ushers us into the Father's presence.

ARE YOU AFRAID TO DIE?

Without a doubt, death is the most dreaded event in our culture. We try hard to cover it over with all kinds of things. Expensive caskets, lots of flowers, polite-language metaphors, and humorous stories are just some of the ways we employ. One man said when his wife died, "Let's have lots of flowers to try to make this thing look as good as we can." We do everything we can think of to escape death. Some people are prepared to pay any price just to prolong life for another week or two.

A Fort Lauderdale, Florida, cancer patient heard his grim prognosis and launched a new business. In a regional magazine advertisement he offered, for a price, to carry messages from survivors to people who were already dead. He received dozens of responses. Messages ranged from a widow's "I love you and will join you soon" message to her deceased husband to "Why, Dad?" from a son who found out too late his father had disinherited him.

Does thinking about dying fill you with fear? Not long ago, we journeyed from Jerusalem, Israel, to Cairo, Egypt, by tour bus. It was a long and interesting trip. Because of political tensions between the two countries, we were driven to the Israeli border check-point by one representative of our tour company and greeted at the Egyptian check-point by a different agent. Our Israeli tour representative pointed across no-man's land at a man in a dark blue suit. He waved. The other man waved back at him. "That man," the Israeli said, "is waiting for you to cross over. Once you are there, he will take good care of you." So it is with death for Christians. Someone waits to greet us just across the way. Once we cross over, he will take good care of us. His name is Jesus Christ. Because of him, death no longer holds any fear for us.

For years, Dr. E. H. Hamilton served Christ faithfully as a missionary to China. After he retired from his overseas work, he returned to America and often called to encourage and inspire me in my ministry. He gave me this poem, which he wrote about death's fears:

Afraid? Of what?
To feel the spirit's glad release?
To pass from pain to perfect peace?
The strife and strain of life to cease?
Afraid? Of that?

Afraid? Of what?
Afraid to see the Savior's face?
To hear his welcome, and to trace
The glory gleam from wounds of grace?
Afraid? Of that?

Afraid? Of what?
A flash? A crash? A pierced heart?
Darkness? Light? Oh, heaven's art!
A wound of his a counterpart!
Afraid? Of that?

Afraid? Of what?
To enter heaven's rest?
And yet to serve the Master blest,
From service good to service best?
Afraid? Of that?

Afraid? Of what?
To do by death what life could not;
Baptize with blood a stony plot,
'Til souls shall blossom from the spot?
Afraid? Of that? [29]

Through his death and resurrection, Jesus taught us an astounding truth about physical death. Not only is it a fear robbed of its terror-filled sting, death itself is dead. It no longer exists for us. The Apostle Paul boldly proclaims this throughout his writings. The non-Christian world describes death with such metaphors as "The Grim Reaper," "The Dark Marauder," "The King of Terrors," or some other such ominous terms. For Paul, and for all Christians, death becomes a synonym for sleep: *"We shall not all sleep, but we shall all be changed" (1 Corinthians 15:51). "If we believe that Jesus died and rose again, even so them also which sleep in Jesus will God bring with him" (1 Thessalonians 4:14).*

What happens when a Christian dies? The Bible says that when we die our souls go instantly to heaven. *"We are always confident, knowing that, whilst we are at home in the body, we are absent from the Lord: We are confi-*

dent, I say, and willing rather to be absent from the body, and to be present with the Lord" (2 Corinthians 6,8). Our bodies, on the other hand, remain on planet Earth until the resurrection, when "the Lord himself shall descend from heaven with a shout, with the voice of the archangel, and with the trump of God: and the dead in Christ shall rise first: Then we which are alive and remain shall be caught up together with them in the clouds, to meet the Lord in the air: and so shall we ever be with the Lord" (1 Thessalonians 4:16,17).

A young preacher tried to illustrate this resurrection truth at the first funeral he conducted. "Folks," he said confidently, "what we have here is just the shell. The nut is no longer in it!"

What happens when people who are not Christians die? Something altogether different. Once again, we let the Bible speak for itself. John, in the Revelation, sets a clear contrast. There are two places where people spend eternity, he writes: "He that overcometh shall inherit all things; and I will be his God, and he shall be my son. But the fearful, and unbelieving, and the abominable, and murderers, and whoremongers, and sorcerers, and idolaters, and all liars, shall have their part in the lake which burneth with fire and brimstone: which is the second death" (Revelation 21:7, 8).

That is it! There are only two options. Either we spend eternity as God's beloved children with Christ in the Father's house of many mansions or separate from God without hope of reconciliation for all eternity. That is why we settle no more important issue in this life than the question of where we will go at death.

A legend tells of a tiny robin clinging to a limb on a giant oak tree while a gale howled all around it. The little bird was singing loudly, seemingly unruffled and undaunted. Even when the storm tore away some roof shingles, the little bird watched and sang. Suddenly the wind ripped a limb off the giant oak tree just above the little bird's head. The limb fell to the ground with a heavy thud. The little bird looked down and made note of where the limb was lying. Suddenly he raised his voice in a new song composed to tease the howling wind: "Go ahead. Blow me off, if you dare, for I have my wings and I'll just ride you to safety. You can't hurt me no matter how hard you try!" Because God's Son, Jesus, took death's sting for us, we can sing to death in chorus with that tiny robin: "Go ahead. Blow me off, if you dare, for I still have my wings and I'll just ride you to safety. You can't hurt me no matter how hard you try!" "I believe in the resurrection of the body!" Do you? I believe it because of the resurrection of the Lord Jesus Christ: "Now is Christ risen from the dead, and become the firstfruits of them that slept" (1 Corinthians 15:20).

THE BIGGEST QUESTION

"I believe in the resurrection of the body and the life everlasting." Dateline NBC reported the true story of an adventuresome young man, full of life, who hired a pilot to fly him to a remote region in Alaska's desolate far north. He told friends and family he was going there to find himself among the natural beauty and mysteries of that place. He prepared for months in advance of his journey. He purchased almost 500 rolls of film and more than 1,400 pounds of provisions. He bought a whole carton of notebooks, which he planned to use as diaries. After arriving at his planned campsite, he recorded his adventures and experiences day by day. He started with vivid descriptions of scenes of unsurpassed splendor. The land was even more beautiful than he ever imagined it would be, he said. None of the descriptions he had read before did it justice. He carefully documented every photograph he took with details of where it was and what it was about. He described the meals he ate and the animals that occasionally came by to finish off his leftovers. Suddenly, one day the whole tenor of his writing changed. He had come face-to-face with an awful discovery. Something terrible gripped his mind. As he noted his diminishing food and film supplies, he realized that in all his careful planning, he had overlooked one vitally important detail: There was no provision for his return to civilization. He was stranded. With no means of communication with the outside world, he had no way of raising any alarm about his predicament. There was no airplane ordered for the return trip, and he had told no one how long he expected to stay in the wilderness. Soon afterward, he noted with sadness that all his food was finished. In frightening words, he recorded his fears after eating his final meal. He wrote, "I should have used more foresight. I should have planned for my departure. I'm so sorry." From that point on, the focus of his diary entries moves from the splendor of untouched natural beauty to the helpless fears and unquenchable hunger pangs of an otherwise bright young man dying slowly in an unnamed valley 225 miles northeast of Fairbanks. A once promising life was coming to a lonely close. Beautiful pictures! Striking descriptions of the wild Alaskan frontier! Fine cameras! All these things lay beside his emaciated, frozen body when a search team discovered it many months later. *"Man dieth, and wasteth away: yea, man giveth up the ghost, and where is he?" (Job 14:10).*

Have you planned your way out? Each chapter in this book looks at great life questions. I have saved the biggest question until now: Have you planned your way out? There are, when we think about it, only five possible answers to the question of what shall happen to us after our existence on Earth is over.

The first answer to the question of what happens when we die is that death is the end. "As a dog dies, so dies a person." Where do dead people go? The hard, cold materialist says, "If you can't show me, I won't believe it." He concludes that the dead are nowhere because no one he knows has been to the other side of death and returned. At his funeral it might be said, "Earth to earth! Ashes to ashes! Dust to dust! That's all, folks! Goodbye!"

The second answer to this most important question of all is that there is nothing to say. Ask the pure scientist what happens after death and the reply is that silence declares that we do not, so far, know the answer. Many great scientists would disagree, of course. Michael Faraday first recognized the power and potential of electricity. Long before that discovery, however, Michael Faraday made a far more powerful one. The great scientist learned that God raised Jesus Christ, his Son, from the dead. Gregor Mendel, who uncovered the earliest principles of genetics, understood all his scientific discoveries to be further revelations of God's existence. He was a dedicated disciple of Jesus. For these and many other leaders in the scientific disciplines, science and theology are not adversaries but complimentary friends. One merely uncovers what the primary focus of the other created. Of things that cannot be proven, however, the pure scientist stays silent. At his funeral, stay silent!

The third possibility is that there is no answer. Ask the atheist and he will tell you that there is no answer. In our generation of Americans, no name is more identified with this position than that of Madelyn Murray O'Hair. Her fierce commitment to absolute unbelief was the catalyst for the banning of Christian prayer and principles from America's public schools. Even more detrimental, however, was Robert Ingersoll, her philosophical hero. He wrote not long before he died, "Every cradle asks us whence and every coffin whither!" [30] It was Ingersoll's way of saying death is a step into the great unknown. At his funeral say, "I just don't know."

The fourth possibility is reincarnation. The new age has rediscovered this ancient Hindu notion in which many in our spiritually floundering generation are investing their eternal hope. It runs counter to everything Jesus Christ stands for. Its whole foundation is the notion of self-salvation: "We can make our own gods and save ourselves!" It says the reward or punishment of the next life is determined solely by what one does in this life. So, the Hindu from whom the new age borrows its foundational principles, reveres cattle over starving people because he believes that Brahman are evil ancestors being punished for this life's failures. This is their second chance at life. At his funeral say, *"It is appointed unto men once to die" (Hebrews 9:27).*

There is but one other possibility. It is that set forth by Jesus Christ, who says, *"God so loved the world, that he gave his only begotten Son, that whosoever believeth in him should not perish, but have everlasting life" (John 3:16),* and, *"I am the resurrection, and the life: he that believeth in me, though he were dead, yet shall he live: And whosoever liveth and believeth in me shall never die" (John 11:25,26).* When he says these things, Christ is either the greatest imposter who ever lived and who has, through these and other promises, misled millions of people; or, he is a lunatic with a messiah complex; or, he is indeed the only Lord of heaven and Earth.

We must each decide for ourselves upon which of these five options we will stake our whole eternity. This much we know: We live in a dying world and no one gets out of it alive. Dead trees in our forests, rotting vegetation on a compost heap, lifeless animals by the roadside, archeological digs among the remnants of former cultures, all these tell us that life, as we know it in this world, is not intended to last forever.

ETERNITY IN OUR HEARTS!

There is a yearning in every human heart to know what happens after death. Why? Because God has put eternity in our hearts (see *Ecclesiastes 3:11*). Ever since *"The LORD God formed man of the dust of the ground, and breathed into his nostrils the breath of life; and man became a living being" (Genesis 2:7),* men and women have yearned to know the answer this final great *Life Line* addresses. Only Jesus Christ satisfies and confirms this universal human yearning for a certain and satisfying eternity.

"The life everlasting" is too real, too essential to what it means to be human not to be true. Therefore, we must believe in it. One heartbeat away from where you are when you read these words—just one breath away—there is a life to come. That is why it is necessary and urgent that you settle this matter now once and for all time. Have you planned your way out?

How can we plan our exit from this world? Jesus tells a gripping story of a man who succeeded by every standard this world calls successful: *"The ground of a certain rich man brought forth plentifully: And he thought within himself, saying, What shall I do, because I have no room where to bestow my fruits? And he said, This will I do: I will pull down my barns, and build greater; and there will I bestow all my fruits and my goods. And I will say to my soul, Soul, thou hast much goods laid up for many years; take thine ease, eat, drink, and be merry. But God said unto him, Thou fool, this night thy soul shall be required of thee: then whose shall those things be, which thou hast provided?" (Luke 12:16-20).*

The man described in this parable was incredibly ordinary in some ways. His friends probably considered him a nice fellow by all the usual standards. Obviously, his financial planner (assuming he had one) would be pleased. He was a good businessman. He was on an expansion program. The Bible hints at no immorality about him. Nor, does it suggest in any way that he was a crook. He certainly provided for his family's long-term welfare. Yet, there was one area where he failed and for that alone Jesus labels him a "Fool." What was so wrong was that he forgot he had a soul to save. Like the young man in Alaska, he neglected to make plans for his way out.

"How shall we escape, if we neglect so great salvation?" (Hebrews 2:3). How do we make sure of the life everlasting? Only through acknowledging that we cannot save ourselves and receiving Christ as Lord. "As it is appointed unto men once to die, but after this the judgment: So Christ was once offered to bear the sins of many; and unto them that look for him shall he appear the second time without sin unto salvation" (Hebrews 9:27,28). The truth is that God loves you and wants to help you in your life. He longs for you to get to know him better through a disciplined program of regular Bible reading and prayer. He promises that when you do you will come to experience the eternal peace, joy, and life that is only possible through his Son, Jesus.

Are you ready to live your life on a higher plane? You can step up to new life in Jesus Christ simply by praying this prayer or one of your own like it:

Dear God, I admit I need your help. My life is empty and uncertain in spite of all I have. I am guilty of ignoring you and of making you compete with idols of my own making. Please come into my life and make me the person you want me to be. I give you control of my life right now. I believe your son, Jesus, died to bring me back to you. Thank you, Father, for loving me that much. In Christ's name, Amen.

If you have prayed this prayer, Jesus Christ is your way out to eternal life with him in heaven. Now you can say with confidence and integrity,

I Believe
In God the Father Almighty,
Maker of heaven and earth.

I Believe
In Jesus Christ, his only Son, our Lord,
who was conceived by the Holy Spirit,
and born of the virgin Mary.
He suffered under Pontius Pilate,
was crucified, died, and was buried;
he descended into hell.
The third day he rose again from the dead.
He ascended into heaven
and sits at the right hand of God the Father almighty.
From there, he will come to judge the living and the dead.

I Believe
In the Holy Spirit,
the holy catholic church,
the communion of saints,
the forgiveness of sins,
the resurrection of the body and the life everlasting,
Amen.

[1] C. S. Lewis, *A Grief Observed,* p. 25. New York: Bantam (1976).

[2] Published by Ambassador-Emerald International, 1999.

[3] *Newsweek,* July 20, 1998.

[4] *Scientific Evidence for the Existence of God,* by Walter Bradley. Published in *The Real Issue,* September/October 1994 (Vol 12, No 3), pp. 3-6.

[5] For more information about the particular names and characteristics of some of the more prevalent Baals, see *International Standard Bible Encyclopedia* Volume 1 (1956), Grand Rapids: Wm. B. Eerdmans Publishing Co.

[6] Charles R. Swindoll, *Encourage Me,* pp. 45, 46. Grand Rapids: Zondervan Publishing House (1982).

[7] Quoted in *God Lite,* by James Edwards. *Christianity Today,* April 29, 1991, pp. 30-31.

[8] Some ideas presented in this chapter are adapted from publications available from Institute for Creation Research, PO Box 2667, El Cajon, CA 92921.

[9] C.S. Lewis, *Mere Christianity,* bk II, ch 3, pp. 55f, New York: MacMillan (1952).

[10] Westminster Shorter Catechism.

[11] *The Heidelberg Catechism,* Question 1 and part of its answer.

[12] *The Shorter Catechism,* Atlanta: John Knox Press, undated, p. 3

[13] Quoted in Michael Williams, Morganfield, *Kentucky Leadership,* Vol. 5, no. 4.

[14] See Donald W. McCullough, *The Trivialization of God,* Colorado Springs: Navpress (1995).

[15] Randy Alcorn, quoted in *Leadership* magazine, vol. 9, no. 1.

[16] Stuart Briscoe, *Choices For A Lifetime,* p. 23. Wheaton: Tyndale House Publishers, (1995).

[17] Dietrich Bonnhoeffer, *The Cost of Discipleship,* translated by R.H. Fuller. New York: The Macmillan Company (1957).

[18] The swoon theory asserts that Jesus did not die but merely fainted and was revived later by the disciples.

[19] Quoted in *Can We Be Good Without Hell?* by Jerry Walls, *Christianity Today,* June 16, 1997 (vol. 41, No. 7) pp. 22-27.

[20] Adapted from *Jane Eyre* by Charlotte Bronte and quoted by Philip Ryken in *Window on the World,* June 30, 1996, p. 2.

[21] Ravi Zacharias, *The Lostness of Humankind,"* in *Preaching Today,* Tape no. 118.

[22] C.S. Lewis, *The Great Divorce,* pp. 123, 124. New York: Macmillan (1946).

[23] Kenneth Woodward, *"Is God Listening?" Newsweek,* March 31, 1997.

[24] J.I. Packer, *Your Father Loves You. Christianity Today,* Vol. 40, No. 4.

[25] C.S. Lewis, *Mere Christianity,* bk II, chap. 5, p. 64. New York: Macmillan (1952).

[26] Alan Redpath, *The Life of Victory,* p. 368. London: Marshall Pickering (1991).

[27] For a further explanation on this and for a more detailed look at the life and work of the Holy Spirit, see my book *The Breath of Abundant Life,* Greenville and Belfast: Ambassador-Emerald International, (1999). Some of the ideas contained in this chapter are adapted from that volume.

[28] Horatio G. Spafford, 1873.

[29] Used by permission from Dorothy Hamilton.

[30] From an undated printed sermon entitled *Life Beyond the Grave,* by Clarence Edward Macartney.

Dr. Robert Leslie Holmes

Born in Belfast, Northern Ireland, Robert Leslie Holmes immigrated to the United States more than thirty years ago. He became a United States citizen five years later.

He earned his Bachelor of Arts degree at the University of Mobile (Alabama), his Master's of Divinity at Reformed Theological Seminary, and his Doctorate from Columbia Theological Seminary. He also has an honorary Doctor of Laws degree from Grove City College, Pennsylvania.

Dr. Holmes has a national reputation as a preacher, author, and motivational speaker to corporate America. He has lectured and spoken at conferences, universities, and churches around the world. This is his sixth book. Prior to being named Senior Minister of First Presbyterian Church of Pittsburgh, PA, he served churches in Mississippi, Georgia, Florida, and California.

He may be reached at:

First Presbyterian Church
320 Sixth Avenue
Pittsburgh, PA 15222

Telephone #412/471-3436
E-mail: rlesholmes@aol.com